"In a moment of great crisis in the Church, in which all the gifts of which St Alphonsus Maria de' Liguori shone seem canceled, discredited and derided by modern clerics and prelates, Stephen Kokx shows us how holiness, which finds in God his own life-giving principle and his own ultimate goal, is the Christian's only way of being, the only possible way to Heaven. This book allows us to rediscover the relevance of the example of St Alphonsus and the perpetual youth of the Church of Christ: let us strip ourselves of the old man, therefore, and put on the new man."—Archbishop Carlo Maria Viganò, Former Apostolic Nuncio to the United States

"It has been said that St Alphonsus de' Liguori took the spiritual principles of St Teresa of Avila and St John of the Cross and made them understandable to the average person on the street. Stephen Kokx does something similar: starting with his own experience, he shows how St Alphonsus' teachings can be applied to life in the 21st century."—Fr Alphonsus Maria Krutsinger, CSSR

SAINT ALPHONSUS FOR THE 21ST CENTURY

SAINT ALPHONSUS FOR THE 21ST CENTURY

A HANDBOOK FOR HOLINESS

by
Stephen Kokx

Printed in the United States of America
© 2023 Stephen Kokx
St Peter's Press

Please send inquiries to
StPetersPress@proton.me

ISBN 979-8-9877771-4-5 (Hardcover)
ISBN 979-8-9877771-0-7 (Paperback)
ISBN 979-8-9877771-1-4 (e-Book)

Cover design by Michael Schrauzer
Typesetting by Kenneth Lieblich

For the salvation of souls.

"Feed my sheep"

ACKNOWLEDGMENTS

This book could not have been written without the assistance of the Holy Spirit. Nor could it have been completed without help from the Blessed Virgin Mary, St Augustine, St Thomas Aquinas, and, of course, St Alphonsus Liguori, to whom I prayed frequently during the writing process. A special thanks is due to Alex Barbas, Kenneth Lieblich, and Michael Schrauzer for making this book a reality. Archbishop Viganò and Fr Krutsinger are also greatly appreciated for having lent their endorsements. The following individuals provided insights on pre-publication drafts and on other aspects of this project, and deserve recognition: Aaron Shanlian, Bill Bjork, Daniel Fredricks, Daniel Vasko, Evan Stambaugh, Greg VanderWoude, Marissa Brand, PH.D, Mark Pestana, PH.D, Mike Austin, Ryan Coffey, Sean Johnson, Sean McCormack, and Stephanie Mader. Additional thanks are extended to those who have helped me, and continue to help me, on my spiritual journey, including Fr Steven Webber, my parents Dave and Cindy Kokx, Tyler Nethercott, and many, many others, especially all the priests who have heard my confessions and administered Holy Communion to me.

CONTENTS

INTRODUCTION

I can't remember the first time I heard about St Alphonsus. I imagine it was in the 1990s while I was attending Sacred Heart of Jesus, the grade school located around the corner from my parents' house in Grand Rapids, Michigan. I'm certain Sister Frances Marie (or one of the other half-dozen School Sisters of Notre Dame who taught me there) mentioned him at some point, but I haven't the slightest recollection of when that took place.

It wasn't until I was twenty-six years old in 2013 that our paths crossed again. At the time, I was living with a friend fifteen minutes away from the Polish-Catholic neighborhood I grew up in. I moved into his house around Christmastime and noticed he had a stack of books, about a foot tall, all written by this still largely unknown-to-me saint. I was slowly making my way back from being a fallen-away Catholic just three short years earlier in college, and still couldn't explain to others—especially Protestants—why they should be Catholic. I figured St Alphonsus could help me re-learn the faith I'd been brought up with.

From the moment I opened those first pages on that cold winter night in January, I was hooked. The beautiful prose, the profound insights, and constant references to Scripture and Church Fathers left me dumbfounded. "Where has this been my entire life?" I wondered in anger. "Why don't priests speak like this anymore? When did the Church stop teaching this?"

St Alphonsus' writings on confession and the priesthood were the first two topics I read. His wisdom on Eucharistic adoration was also something I came across early on. As you'll discover in this book, my life drastically changed after those initial encounters, but only because I was earnestly seeking the truth and was willing to let God live in me.

I soon found myself swimming in an ocean of supernatural wisdom I never knew existed. Previously, my spiritual life amounted to little more than praying the Our Father, Hail Mary, and Glory Be. I hardly went to confession and foolishly believed that when it was difficult to pray, God was angry with me. Like a lot of Catholics today (or so it seems), I was also under the impression that I just needed to go to church on Sunday to get into Heaven.

I spent night after night for months on end that winter soaking up as much as I could from those books. I took diligent notes and used a highlighter to emphasize the most important sections. Sometimes, entire pages ended up bright yellow. Fortunately for my roommate, I'd purchased my own set by then. To say the least, his remained in much better condition than mine, which today are missing their covers and have dozens of pages unglued from the binding. A small price to pay for spiritual advancement!

The devil was not unaware of the progress I was making. Nor was he ignorant of the growth my roommate was experiencing. It didn't take long for him to make his displeasure known to us.

On a chilly February night, my roommate was praying the Rosary in the living room. He had just finished his last Hail Mary when a loud *thud* from the upstairs bedroom came crashing down. A crack, nearly a foot long, immediately appeared in the ceiling. On a different occasion, his phone began dialing (666) 666-6666 over and over again. Another time, the DVD player beneath the television set kept opening and closing, despite the power being off.

I myself was targeted as well. On every Sunday night for a month straight during Lent that year, a cold breeze flowed through my room as if the window was open. There was a noticeable temperature drop that wasn't present any other time of the day. I also heard tearing noises coming from the ceiling when I was trying to sleep. It was as if duct tape was being put on and then ripped off every thirty seconds. Meanwhile, the blinds next to my bed sounded like someone was running their fingers up and down, flicking each one along the way. What's more, my missal and Rosary would end up on the desk across my room despite being on the nightstand near my bed the evening before.

Although I was rather frightened when these experiences began, after praying to St Alphonsus, I realized that the devil was only able to do these things because God was allowing him to. Satan has no power of his own, I came to better understand. Just like in the story of Job, he can assault us but only if God permits it.

Eventually, whenever these interactions took place, I would say out loud, after much prayer and preparation, "God is letting you do this, Satan. You don't scare me. God is in control of you and won't let anything happen that will harm my soul. Whatever you think you are doing, God is letting it occur for a greater purpose."

My roommate and I eventually asked a priest to perform an exorcism. Thankfully, everything stopped after that. The lesson I took away from it all was that the devil is limited in what he can do to us, especially if we've been praying and are in a state of grace. As Psalms 23:4 says, "Though I should walk in the midst of the shadow of death, I will fear no evil, for Thou art with me."

Looking back, this was the first real combat I had with the devil. Up until then, he didn't need to do anything. I was right where he wanted me—living in sin and spiritually aloof. Despite being cast out of that house, he didn't raise the white flag in surrender just yet. As I would only learn in the years that followed, this was merely his first volley in a war that has lasted until the present day and will continue until my dying breath. To be completely honest, I haven't won every battle he and I have had since then. In fact, I've lost quite a few. I'll speak about those later in this book.

As winter gave way to spring, I decided I couldn't keep what I was learning to myself. I soon gathered St Alphonsus' most insightful remarks and arranged them according to theme. I eventually turned them into a lecture I called, simply, "The Spiritual Teachings of St Alphonsus." I presented that at the Diocese of Grand Rapids' Catechetical Conference later that year. About thirty-five middle-aged youth ministers, teachers, and pastoral associates were in attendance. Almost all of them gave me exceedingly positive reviews. One elderly gentleman told me I should consider becoming a priest. A woman in her sixties excitedly said, "More people need to hear this!" I'm sure she'd be happy to learn that this book is a direct result of that presentation.

Though born in the seventeenth century, St Alphonsus can and should be revisited by Catholics today, if for nothing else than the simple fact that spiritual wisdom is never obsolete due to the persistent effects of Original Sin. Submitting oneself to St Alphonsus, a Doctor of the Church, is a surefire way to live a holy life.

Another reason Catholics today should reacquaint themselves with him is because he's uniquely suited for our times. Among other things, St Alphonsus evangelized the poor and those who were considered to be on the fringes of society—farmers, country folk, and others who would have been more or less uneducated. "He came from the nobility, but cherished the poor and lived as one of them," one biography said of him.[1]

The way I see it, Catholics today are in a similar situation, but instead of being poor monetarily they're poor spiritually, having been deprived of the inexhaustible riches of the Church's traditions. As a result, Catholics in the 21st century are woefully

---

1 Christopher Rengers, OFM Cap and Matthew Bunson, KHS, *The 35 Doctors of the Church: Revised Edition* (Charlotte, NC: TAN Books, 2014), 666.

unfamiliar with the great treasures their faith has to offer. Who better to give them than St Alphonsus?

I purposefully don't spend much time in this book on the life of St Alphonsus, as there already exists plenty of resources available on that subject. Still, it's important to have some knowledge about who he was as a person.

Alphonsus Mary Anthony John Francis Cosmas Damian Michael Gaspar de' Liguori was born on September 27, 1696. The oldest of eight children, he hailed from a noble family in the Kingdom of Naples. His father, Don Joseph Liguori, was a naval officer and captain of the royal galleys. His mother, the Spanish Anna Catherine Cavalieri, was a pious homemaker who dutifully raised Alphonsus and his siblings in the Catholic faith. She performed her duties so marvelously that aside from Alphonsus, his brothers Cajetan and Anthony also gave themselves to God in religious life. Two of his sisters—Mary Louise and Mary Anne—became nuns. Alphonsus' other siblings, Theresa and Hercules (with whom he was closest), entered the married state. Magdalen died during infancy.

Being the first-born male, St Alphonsus followed the path laid out for him by his ambitious father. During his youth, he received instruction from private tutors in an array of subjects, including music, drawing, and architecture. At the age of sixteen, he earned civil and canon law degrees, though he didn't start practicing until several years later. A talented jurist, Alphonsus excelled in his profession, making many influential connections. On more than two occasions, his father sought to arrange for him to be married.

At the age of twenty-seven in 1723, Alphonsus lost an important court case. At issue was a land dispute involving the Grand Duke of Tuscany. Although Alphonsus meticulously prepared and carefully argued his case, the judge readily sided against him, ruling in favor of his opponents, the famed Medici legal team.

While it has long been believed that Alphonsus lost due to an oversight on his part, recent scholarship suggests political pressure and even bribery involving a high-ranking Cardinal influenced the outcome ahead of time. "World, I know thee now. Courts, you never shall see me again!" Alphonsus is believed to have said at the time.[2][3]

In August of that same year, Don Joseph instructed his son to accompany him to an event at the royal palace in honor of the wife of Holy Roman Emperor Charles VI. Instead of joining him, Alphonsus told his father that the gathering was "nothing but vanity." Upset at his son's reluctance, Don Joseph scolded him. "Oh, do what you like!"

It was around this time that Alphonsus visited a nearby hospital to tend to the sick. While there, he heard a voice say to him, "Leave the world and give thyself entirely to Me." Although he was startled at first, he humbly replied: "Lord Jesus, too long have I resisted Thy grace; do with me what Thou will." He also went to the nearby Church of Our Lady of Ransom. While there, he took out his sword—a symbol of his noble patronage—and laid it on the altar of Mary, vowing then and there to give His life to God as a priest.

When Alphonsus' father discovered his son's intention to enter the priesthood (something he had been considering in secret for several years prior) he did everything he could to stop it. "I pray God to take either myself or you out of the world, for I cannot bear the sight of you," he supposedly said. But Alphonsus' earthly father could not prevent the will of Alphonsus' Heavenly Father from being carried out. After completing his seminary studies at his parents' house three years later, Alphonsus was

2 Frederick Jones, ed., "Alphonsus de Liguori: Selected Writings," in *The Classics of Western Spirituality*, (Mahwah, NJ: Paulist Press, 1999), 18.
3 Frederick Jones, *Alphonsus de Liguori: Saint of Bourbon Naples, 1696-1787* (Liguori, MO: Liguori Publications,1992), 35–38.

ordained a priest at the age of thirty on December 21, 1726. For the next five years, he engaged in missionary work in the Naples area for the Congregation for Apostolic Missions. He taught on street corners, held outdoor meetings for the poor, and organized gatherings for laity in their homes during the evenings. He even had hopes of traveling to China.

During his priesthood, St Alphonsus encountered many obstacles. When all but one of his initial companions abandoned him, nearby residents sneered at him for leaving behind the success he had been having in the world. Undeterred, Alphonsus pressed on. Known for his simple and direct preaching style, he won many admirers, even his own father.

In November 1732, St Alphonsus founded the Congregation of the Most Holy Redeemer, also known as the Redemptorist Order. Redemptorists specialize in conducting retreats and engaging in missionary activity to the most abandoned souls. In total, three Redemptorists other than Alphonsus have been declared saints: St Gerard Majella (1726–55), St Clement Hofbauer (1751–1820), and St John Neumann (1811–60). Sr Maria Celeste (1696–1755), the founder of the Redemptoristine Nuns, was declared Blessed in 2016. More than a half dozen other Redemptorists have been awarded that title as well.

During his lifetime, St Alphonsus published over one hundred books, essays, and short treatises on spiritual, moral, and doctrinal topics. He ministered to earthquake victims, painted, and even composed poems and songs, some of which are still popular in Italy today. Although his first significant work wasn't published until his late forties, he is believed to be among the best-selling authors of all-time due to the vast number of volumes, re-printings, and translations that have been done with his works.[4]

Some of St Alphonsus' most well-known books include *Visits to the Most Blessed Sacrament and the Blessed Virgin Mary,*

4 Rengers & Bunson, 659–660.

The Glories of Mary, The True Spouse of Jesus Christ (which was written for nuns), and *The Dignities and Duties of the Priest.* His *Preparation for Death, Sermons for all the Sundays in the Year,* and *Moral Theology* are also widely popular, as is *The Way of the Cross,* which is used by Catholics around the word during Fridays in Lent to commemorate Our Lord's Passion. Known for being eminently readable and intensely practical, Alphonsus' writings—aside from leading souls to intimate union with God—also helped defeat the Jansenist heresy.

In 1762, at the age of sixty-six, St Alphonsus was appointed—against his will—Bishop of the Diocese of St Agatha of the Goths in Southern Italy. As he aged, he suffered many ailments, including rheumatoid arthritis and a curved spine that confined him to a wheelchair during the last years of his life. He regularly informed those who wrote to him of his illnesses, often predicting that his death was not far off. He eventually went to his eternal reward in 1787. Fifty-two years later, in 1839, he was canonized a saint by Pope Gregory XVI. In 1871, he was declared a Doctor of the Church by Blessed Pope Pius IX. Today, he is revered as the patron saint of moral theologians and confessors.

It is in the missionary spirit of St Alphonsus and of the Redemptorist Order that I have written this book. If it had not been for his intervention in my life when I was a younger man, I may very well not be a practicing Catholic today. In no way am I seeking to provide a comprehensive overview of all of St Alphonsus' writings. Rather, my aim is to present, in a succinct and direct manner, some of what I believe are his most helpful teachings for Catholics in the modern age, while also sharing personal anecdotes about how they have benefited and continue to benefit me on my own journey. My goal is that this book will help you navigate the world around you and save your soul. St Alphonsus changed my own life. He will undoubtedly change yours. The

Church in the 21st century is in desperate need of the timeless wisdom St Alphonsus provides. I pray She will rediscover it.

Stephen Kokx
Feast of St Alphonsus
August 2023

CHAPTER 1

PERFECTION

"Be perfect like your Father in Heaven is perfect." These are the words of Our Lord and Savior Jesus Christ in the Gospel of Matthew.[5]

But how can you and I, mere mortal human beings who, even at our best (according to the Book of Proverbs) sin seven times a day, come anywhere close to being like God?[6] After all, He's not only all-powerful and all-just, but all-knowing and all-loving as well. Answering that question is at the heart of the spiritual writings of St Alphonsus Liguori.

When people hear the word perfection, they take it to mean "impeccable" or "to be without flaw." It goes without saying that Christ wants us to not offend Him. But He also understands that we're broken creatures scarred by Original Sin, and that no one can go through life without failing in the spiritual life in some way, shape, or form. St Peter himself, the apostle Our Lord gave the keys of Heaven to, denied he even knew Him, and not only once, but on three separate occasions.

According to St Alphonsus, being perfect occurs when we make ourselves one with God. Perfection is "founded entirely on the love of God," he writes. "Perfect love of God ... consists

---

5 Matthew 5:48
6 Proverbs 24:16: "For a just man shall fall seven times and shall rise again: but the wicked shall fall down into evil."

in uniting" our will with God's Will. The more one "unites his will with the Divine Will, the greater will be his love of God."

Several fairly obvious questions should arise when reflecting on these remarks. How can we "unite our wills" to God's Will? What *is* God's Will? And how do we actually *show* God we love Him? The answers to these questions—and ones similar to them—are both simple and complex and are the focus of this book.

Thy Will Be Done

St Alphonsus lays out several important steps for those who are seeking to be perfect.

First, he teaches that they should refrain from expressions that indicate opposition to the Will of God. They should abstain from saying things like, "What intolerable heat! What horrible cold!… or other words expressive of repugnance to the Will of God. We ought to will everything to be as it is, since God is He who orders it all."

Second, Christians mustn't be angry with the "hunger, thirst, poverty, desolation, or disgrace" they experience. Rather, they should say, "Lord, be it Thine to make and to unmake. I am content" with whatever you desire for me.

Third, St Alphonsus says that those who are striving to be perfect shouldn't be disturbed by any natural defect they may have—a bad memory, for instance, or "slowness of apprehension, mean abilities, a crippled limb, or weak health." Let us "thank God for what, in His pure goodness, He has given us." He explains:

> Who knows? Perhaps if God had given us greater talent, better health, a more personable appearance, we might have lost our souls! Great talent and knowledge have caused

many to be puffed up with the idea of their own importance and, in their pride, they have despised others.

St Alphonsus also teaches that those who want to be perfect need to accept corporal infirmities. "We must be particularly resigned [to our ailments] and we must embrace them willingly, both in such a manner, and for such a time, as God wills." We "ought to employ the usual remedies" to heal ourselves, he adds, "but if they do us no good, let us unite ourselves to the Will of God, and this will do us much more good than health." Our virtue is greater "if, in times of sickness, we do not complain of our sufferings."

The Road to Perfection

St Alphonsus is the patron saint of confessors and a Doctor of the Church. He was well aware of the fact that souls don't get to Heaven simply by going to Mass or, as Protestants believe, by professing Christ as the Son of God. How did he know that? Because, as the Epistle of St James states, "a faith without works is dead."[7] Even the devil acknowledges Christ is the Savior of mankind, yet he is damned forever because of his *actions*.

St Alphonsus' extensive writings remind us that our earthly existence is a battle, a never-ending struggle against the world, the flesh, and the devil, and that our combat doesn't end until we draw our last breath. "Our whole life must be one continued contest," he writes. In saying that, he echoes the words of St Paul in his letter to the Philippians: "Work out your salvation with fear and trembling."[8] St Paul spoke in a similar way in his letter to St Timothy: "I have fought the good fight, I have finished the race, I have kept the faith."[9]

7 James 2:26   8 Philippians 2:12   9 2 Timothy 4:7

3

One of the major obstacles to winning "the race" of life is what St Alphonsus calls self-love, which he says comes in two forms—good self-love and bad self-love. Good self-love is "that which makes us seek eternal life." Bad self-love "inclines us to pursue earthly goods, and to prefer them to our everlasting welfare, and to the Holy Will of God."

When we pursue "bad self-love," we distance ourselves from God. This separation makes us miserable. "Unhappy the soul that suffers itself to be ruled by its own inclinations," St Alphonsus observes. On the other hand, when we submit ourselves to God and deny ourselves the comforts this life has to offer, the more joyful we will be. "The less … a Christian desires to indulge their passions, the more he will love God," St Alphonsus says. "If he seeks nothing but God, he will then possess perfect charity."

Dominant Faults

This is all easier said than done! Anyone who's struggled with, as I have, alcohol, gambling, impurity, or any other bad habit knows that quitting certain behaviors can sometimes feel impossible. Relapses are far too common when we try to stop vices we've engaged in for years. "He who sins is a slave to sin," John 8:34 explains.

When it comes to spiritual warfare, each of us has what are called dominant faults. Dominant faults are the one, two, or sometimes three or more types of sins we're tempted to commit pretty much our entire lives. They're the behaviors we struggle with the most … and for the longest time. Pride, gluttony, lust, and sloth are just a few examples of dominant faults.

Unfortunately, many people don't try to correct their dominant faults. They erroneously believe they are what makes them unique, so they give into them without ever thinking they're offending God.

Other times, what happens is that Christians who have tried but have repeatedly failed to overcome their sinful tendencies begin to resent God. They start to blame Him for having made them the way they are, and they wrongly believe they're irreformable. Eventually, they convince themselves they'll never be holy enough to get into Heaven, so they give up on the spiritual life out of despair, like Judas did.

This is the completely wrong approach, for two reasons.

One, God never gives us crosses we can't carry. If you don't like something about yourself—or you have strong inclinations to certain sins—you have to work to overcome them. This life is not easy. In fact, it's a pilgrimage. We're not meant to stay here. "This world is passing away," 1 John 2:17 says. Our home is in Heaven. If we want to enjoy Heaven with Christ, we have to suffer like He did. Christ carried His cross. *We* must carry ours, whatever it may be. No servant is greater than his master.

Two, God has promised to help us resist whatever trials we encounter. "Where sin abounds, grace abounds more," Romans 5:20 states. To be sure, the devil can entice us with many pleasures. And, yes, he can present temptations that can provoke us to indulge in our dominant faults. But at the end of the day, we all have free will. Satan can't force us to sin. It's ultimately up to us to choose good or evil. We alone will be held accountable for our decisions.

St Thomas Aquinas, the greatest philosopher and theologian the Church has ever produced, is a good example of how to fight temptations. When he was a teenager, St Thomas' family didn't like that he wanted to become a Dominican monk. They preferred he join the more prestigious Benedictine order. When he refused to listen, they locked him up in their family castle near the town of Roccasecca, Italy. One night, his brothers sent him a prostitute. At the time, Thomas, a young man, could have easily given in to "bad self-love." But he didn't. He was resolute

5

in his love for God, so much so that he chased the woman away with a flaming piece of wood. He was rewarded by God with the grace of never being tempted to impurity again. Now that's how you combat sin!

Mortification

St Alphonsus knew the dominant faults of many souls. As a priest who spent hours on end in the confessional, he would have heard, week in and week out, the same sins committed by his parishioners. And week in and week out, he undoubtedly would have given them various forms of penance. One type of penance he would have asked them to do is mortification.

"St Francis Borgia says that prayer introduces the love of God into the soul," St Alphonsus writes, "but mortification prepares a place for it by banishing from the heart earthly affections—the most powerful obstacles to charity."

What is mortification? Generally speaking, mortification means self-denial. It is the rejection of that which is pleasurable to the flesh and makes us lazy in the spiritual life. By undertaking mortifications we atone for our sins. Another phrase often used instead of mortification is "dying to self."

According to St Alphonsus, there are two types of mortification: external mortification and internal mortification. External mortification, or the mortification of the senses, consists in "depriving oneself of what is agreeable" to us. It deals with repressing "the appetites of the body in order to bring it under subjection to the spirit." The saints "have endeavored to mortify the flesh continually," he observes. Internal mortification, on the other hand, deals with "the irregular affections of the soul." It consists in subjecting "ambition, inordinate anger, self-esteem, attachment to self-interest, to our own opinion, or to self-will." External mortification without interior self-denial "profits the soul but little," he warns. St Alphonsus teaches there are three ways we can acquire the "spirit of mortification."

The first means is to "discover the passion which premeditates in our heart, and which most frequently leads us into sin" and then "endeavor to conquer it." For some, this may mean recognizing something as simple as their smartphone is how the devil prevents them from living a virtuous life.

The second means to acquire the spirit of mortification is to "resist the passions, and to beat them down before they acquire strength. If one of them becomes strong by habitual indulgence, the subjugation of it will be exceedingly difficult."

The third means is to "endeavor to change the object of our passions, that thus the pernicious and vicious desires of the heart may become salutary and holy."

What St Alphonsus is saying here is that we need to learn what our dominant faults are and realize that the more we allow ourselves to be overcome by them, the harder it will be to resist them in the future. This is especially true of sins of the flesh. St Alphonsus is also imploring us to make a more strenuous effort to turn away from our fleeting impulses and fix our hearts on God alone, our true source of happiness. "Do not follow your own desires," he writes. "Fly from the indulgence of self-will."

During his own life, St Alphonsus took on many external mortifications, including the wearing of sackcloth and placing an iron chain around his neck while eating. He would also add bitter herbs to his food, which he consumed while kneeling. What's more, he limited himself to bread and water on Saturdays in honor of the Blessed Virgin Mary. "That great servant of God, Vincenzo Carafa, of the Society of Jesus, used to say that God has given us earthly goods not only for our delight," St Alphonsus once wrote, but that "we might have a means of showing our gratitude to Him by abstaining from pleasures, and giving Him back His own gifts in proof of our love."

Again, this is easier said than done. Avoiding the bar at happy hour when we know it usually ends up turning into an all-night bender can be a hard habit to break. But if we're serious about our salvation we have no other choice. We must—absolutely must—embrace the spirit of mortification and reject the comforts of this world that lead us into temptation. The sinner "dishonors God" by preferring a "miserable pleasure" to His eternal friendship, St Alphonsus recalls.

To Make Us Saints

Sadly, untold numbers of people will not embrace the spirit of mortification. Instead of staying faithful to Christ's teachings, countless souls will give in to the lies of the devil. This we know from Scripture. "Wide is the gate, and broad is the way that leadeth to destruction, and many there are who go in," Matthew 7:13 tells us.

When Our Lady of Fátima appeared to Jacinta, Francisco, and Lúcia in Portugal in 1917, she told them that more souls go to Hell because of sins of the flesh than for any other reason. Lúcia, who later gave her life to God by becoming a nun, recounted the horrifying vision of Hell that the Blessed Mother shared with them.

> Plunged in this fire were demons and souls in human form, like transparent burning embers, all blackened or burnished bronze, floating about in the conflagration ... falling back on every side like sparks in huge fires, without weight or equilibrium, amid shrieks and groans of pain and despair.[10]

---

10 Bl. Lúcia dos Santos, "The Secret in Three Parts: The First Part," The Fatima Center, n.d., https://fatima.org/about/fatima-the-message/the-secret-in-three-parts-the-first-part/.

Catholics must not give into the most dominant sins that characterize the modern age—gluttony, pornography, sodomy, fornication, abortion, and transgenderism, to name a few. Unfortunately, these abominations are promoted as normal by the media, schools, celebrities, and many prominent politicians, even self-professed Catholic ones.

Catholics today must stand firm in their opposition to these behaviors and recognize, as St Alphonsus did, that God created us to live in these times for our sanctification.

> [God] sends us crosses, not because He wishes evil to us, but because He desires our welfare, and because He knows that they are conducive to our salvation.... Even the chastisements which come from the Lord are not for our destruction, but for our good, and for the correction of our faults.

"In sending us tribulations," St Alphonsus continues, "God intends to make us saints."

Considerations

- Do I pray every day to know God's Will? What do I believe His Will is for me right now? Is the current direction of my life leading me closer to Him or further away?

- Of the recommendations St Alphonsus has for souls seeking to be perfect, which could I most easily implement in my life starting today?

- Which of my behaviors would be considered "bad self-love," according to St Alphonsus? Which forms of "good self-love" can I replace them with?

- What are my dominant faults? When I am tempted by them, do I have recourse to God like St Thomas Aquinas did? How can St Alphonsus' teachings help me overcome at least one of my dominant faults in the next month?

- If I made a list of the mortifications I practice most often, what would be on it? Anything? What are three small acts of self-denial I can perform in the next three days that will help me acquire the "spirit of mortification" spoken about by St Alphonsus?

CHAPTER 2

LOVE OF GOD

St Alphonsus teaches that a soul that loves God is not disturbed by any misfortune that should happen to it. "He that reposes in the Divine Will, is like a man placed above the clouds: he sees the lightning, and hears the claps of thunder and the raging of the tempest below, but he is not injured or disturbed by them."

But you and I know that remaining peaceful is extremely challenging, even when we're in good health and enjoying success. It's far harder when we are sick or suffering from a chronic ailment or life-threatening disease. Loving God, especially when we're not feeling well, can be especially difficult.

When I was in my early thirties, I was battling a mysterious, five-year-long neurological illness. Before then, I was relatively healthy and never had a serious medical issue. It was March of 2018 and I'd been clearing my throat every few minutes on a daily basis for five months straight. I went to the doctor and was given a ten-day round of antibiotics for what was suspected to be an infection. Soon afterwards, my abdomen and left calf began to shake after I ate certain foods. It was a terrifying feeling that caused me to rush to the urgent care center. When I arrived, the nurse drew some blood to make sure nothing serious was happening. "All normal," she said, as I sat there feeling like my body was a tuning fork. Puzzled, I trusted the results and went home.

Over the next several months (and years), my symptoms worsened. Eventually, my gut was violently twitching after every meal. My thigh and calf muscles began pulsating too. Nerves all over my body—feet, lower back, and even chest and arms—felt like they were being pricked with pins and needles. I had no clue what was happening. It was like I was being electrocuted from the inside out. One doctor recommended I take an anti-depressant. "It's all in your head," he said. Another believed my autonomic nervous system was "out of whack," while offering no real solutions other than for me to "de-stress."

I often cursed God as I laid in bed trying to fall asleep for not healing my body. I even demanded He show me He cared for me. "This is how you treat your servants? After all I have done for you?! I've lost friends for defending your teachings! This is seriously how you repay me?! Answer me!"

Suffering for Love

St Alphonsus teaches that when we are experiencing physical sufferings, we should express our love for God all the more. Why? Because illness is "the acid test of spirituality ... it discloses whether our virtue is real or a sham." He goes on:

> If the soul is not agitated, does not break out in lamentations, is not feverishly restless in seeking a cure, but instead is submissive to the doctors and to superiors, is serene and tranquil, completely resigned to God's Will, it is a sign that that soul is well grounded in virtue.

This lesson is most on display in the Old Testament story of Job. Job was a wealthy man who had many honorable things—land, a large family, and a good reputation. With God's permission, the devil was allowed to test Job's fidelity. He was forced to undergo many hardships, including the death of his children. He had boils on his skin as well. After patiently enduring these sufferings and offering penance to God, Job was restored twice over from his previous state in life.

St Alphonsus believes that there are lessons to be learned from Job's life. "Job desired nothing more than to say 'Blessed be God.'" He desired only what pleased God and recognized that all that happens to him, "happens through the Will of God." It was Job, he further writes, who said, "if we have received good things from the hand of God, why should we not receive evil?'"

How many people alive today think like this? How many—instead of praising God for both the good *and bad things* that happen to them—behave like I did when I was sick? Acting with ingratitude and shouting at Him for the sufferings that befall them? Moreover, how many people fail to recognize that Christ not only laid down *His life* for them (a sure sign as any that He loves them) but that God is the source of everything that brings them joy in life, including their job, families, friends, and personal preferences?

St Alphonsus calls on us to thank God for whatever He deigns to give us, even if we might not enjoy it. "In cold and heat, in rain and wind, the soul united to God says: 'I want it to be warm, to be cold, windy, to rain, because God wills it.'"

Growing in Love

In the next chapter, I'll explain how St Alphonsus' writings on suffering helped me overcome the anger I had toward God for letting me get sick. I'll also discuss how I came to embrace the illness He sent me. For now, I'd like to share five recommendations St Alphonsus has for those who want to advance in love for God during their day-to-day lives—and how they can accept that everything that happens to them, even cancer, is for their own good.

In order to grow in love for God, St Alphonsus says we first need to have an ardent desire to unite our will to His Will. "Many are called to perfection," he writes, "they are urged on towards it by grace, they conceive a desire of it; but because they never really resolve to acquire it, they live and die in the ill-odor of their tepid and imperfect life."

After a soul has properly desired perfection, it must renounce all things that do not refer to God. God "will tolerate no rival." St Alphonsus lists love of money, love of material goods, and "every attachment that does not have God as its object" as the primary obstacles to loving Him. "In order to attain to the perfect love of God it is necessary," he continues, "to deny oneself by gladly embracing what is opposed to self-love." God "has a just claim to be alone in His possession ... of a heart created by Himself."

The third step needed to grow in love of God is to embrace humility. Christians can humble themselves in two ways, St Alphonsus says. One way is by humbling their intellect. The other is by humbling their will. "Humility of the intellect is to have a lowly opinion of ourselves and see us as deserving of contempt." The "humble man ... says with Job: 'I have sinned and indeed I have offended, and I have not received what I have deserved.'" Humility of the will, on the other hand, involves the desire to be despised by others and in the pleasure such contempt affords us. "Humility of the will consists in ... taking pleasure in contempt." Some examples of this could be ill-treatment from our superior or boss or being mocked for doing something Christlike. "This good Master loves and enriches with His favors only those ... who embrace humiliations with patience," St Alphonsus writes. Humility of the will is "most meritorious," he adds, "because acts of the will are more pleasing to God than acts of the intellect." St Alphonsus' writings on humility will be discussed later in this chapter.

The fourth means of acquiring love of God according to St Alphonsus is to frequently meditate on the sufferings of Christ. "The Lord once revealed to a pious hermit," he says, "that no devotion was better to enkindle the love of God in the heart than meditation on the sufferings of Christ. It has always been a favorite devotion with the Saints."

Lastly, St Alphonsus teaches that we can advance in love of God simply by praying.

> The constant prayer of a Christian soul must be: 'Jesus, give me Thy holy love; Mary my Mother, obtain for me the love of God; my Guardian Angel and all my holy patrons, intercede for me that I may love my God with my whole heart and soul.' The Lord is generous in the bestowal of His gifts; but He is especially bountiful in giving His love to those who seek it.

Thus, St Alphonsus teaches, "the more one unites his will with the Divine Will, the greater will be his love of God."

Total Abandonment

St Alphonsus' writings on self-denial and love of God overwhelmed me (in a good way) the first time I read them. My entire paradigm shifted literally in a matter of seconds, but only because I was open to having my life changed then and there. My soul immediately understood that my sin-filled life was keeping me from being united with God. Like so many young men today, the main sins I struggled with in my mid- and late-twenties were impurity, gluttony, sloth, and anger. St Alphonsus helped me understand each of these for what they really were: a crime in the eyes of Our Lord.

According to Saint Alphonsus—and the Catholic Church for that matter—sin is the number one obstacle to loving God.

"When the soul consents to mortal sin, she ungratefully says to God: 'Depart from me' ... [for] God cannot remain with sin in the soul," he says.

One of the many tricks the devil uses on young people, and certainly used on me, is to convince them they have a long life ahead of them and that they can seek forgiveness when they're in their seventies or eighties. "Dying is something old people do," I often told myself when I was younger. I foolishly believed that on my deathbed I would ask for forgiveness and that everything would turn out fine. This is a lie, St Alphonsus emphatically states. It is a deceit straight from the depths of Hell. God, he argues, gives us a certain number of sins. Once that threshold has been crossed, His mercy comes to an end.

> It is the opinion of St Basil, St Jerome, St Ambrose, St Augustine, and others, that as God has determined for each one the number of talents, the goods of fortune, and the number of days to be bestowed upon him, so He has also determined for each one the number of sins to be pardoned him, which being completed, God will pour out His chastisements upon him and pardon him no more.

Although God has patience and waits for the sinner, St Alphonsus continues, "when the day arrives for the measure of his sins to be filled up He will wait for him no longer, but chastise him."

The Little Flower

As mentioned in Chapter 1, even zealous souls can struggle to turn from their sinful ways and unite themselves with God. It can sometimes take years to conquer our dominant faults. Many times, they abandon the quest for perfection altogether. The wisdom of St Thérèse of Lisieux (1873–97) is helpful in this regard, as she reinforces St Alphonsus' teaching on abandoning ourselves to God no matter what He has in store for us.

In a booklet entitled *Joy in Suffering*, Bishop Adolph Alexander Noser (1900–81) relates that St Thérèse told the Child Jesus she wanted to give herself unreservedly to Him so she could be His "little plaything." Bishop Noser quotes St Thérèse as having said the following:

> I told [Jesus] not to treat me like a costly toy that children are content to look at without venturing to touch, but rather as He would a little ball of no value, that He might throw to the ground, toss about, pierce, leave in a corner or else press to His Heart if it so please Him.... If He wishes to break His 'little plaything' to pieces, He is quite free to do so; yes, I want only what He wills.[11]

This approach to the spiritual life is in complete alignment with the teachings of St Alphonsus. If "you desire to honor God...consider yourself deserving only of contempt and punishment," he once wrote, being sure to remain humble in all things. Saints sure do think alike, don't they?

Humility

It was mentioned earlier that St Alphonsus holds humility in such high esteem that he considers it a non-negotiable trait for souls striving for perfection. It's worth diving deeper into his thoughts on this subject.

"Humility is called by the saints the foundation and safeguard of all the virtues," he recalls. "If it is not the most prominent among the virtues, it occupies, according to St Thomas, the first

---

11 A.A. Noser, *Joy in Suffering: According to St Therese of the Child Jesus* (Charlotte, NC: TAN Books, 2006), 59.

place as the foundation of the rest." In the spiritual life "humility must precede everything else in order to banish pride, to which God is so opposed."

As previously mentioned, St Alphonsus teaches that humility comes in two forms—humility of the intellect and humility of the will. In his writings, he lays out five rules for those who want to possess this great virtue.

First, we should never boast of anything we do. "When you perceive that you have performed a good work or acquired any virtue, look back at your former [sinful life]; remember what you were, and conclude that all the good that you possess is but an alms from the Almighty."

Second, never confide in your own strength. "Without the Divine Aid you can do nothing... endeavor to live in continual and utter distrust of yourself... the proud man trusts in his own courage, and therefore yields to temptation."

Third, in order to be humble we must never give into anger or despondency.

> Should you be so unfortunate as to commit a fault... humble your soul; repent, and with a stronger sense of your own weakness, throw yourself into the arms of the Lord. To be angry with ourselves after having committed a fault, is not an act of humility, but of pride.

Fourth, in order to be humble, we must never think we are better than others who commit more grievous sins than we do. "Pity [their] misfortune, and trembling for yourself say with holy David: 'Unless the Lord has been my helper, my soul had almost dwelt in hell.'"

Fifth, St Alphonsus says we must consider ourselves the greatest sinner on earth. "They who are truly humble... possess the most perfect knowledge, not only of the divine perfections, but also of their own miseries and sin."

"Humility is called a treasure," St Alphonsus summarizes, "because the Lord sees to it that the humble abound in good things. When man's heart is full of himself, there is no room for God's gifts."

Learning Humility

For five years during my mid and late twenties, I was an adjunct instructor at two community colleges in West Michigan. I taught political science and a "college success course" for first-year students who needed help getting acclimated to higher education. Note-taking skills, how student loans work, and selecting a major were just some of the topics we covered.

My first semester was, admittedly, not great. I was twenty-five years old and fresh out of graduate school. Most of my student evaluations said I was "a nice guy" but others were more critical. "Professor Kokx talks more than he teaches." "He says 'um' way too much."

As a melancholic, I took those comments personally. I immediately took steps to shore up my teaching skills. I bought dozens of books on classroom management and attended professional development courses on how to be an effective educator.

As the years went by I became less interested in what I was doing. I was growing in my faith and wanted to bring souls to Christ instead of teaching them about American government. So I opted to seek work elsewhere. Overall, my time in higher education was an amazing experience. I was able to help hundreds of young people and made tons of memories. I hope I had a lasting impact on their lives in a positive way. I always tried to be fair, firm, but also funny.

When that last semester ended, I took time off to relax but also pray about what I should do next, as I was living in my parents' basement at the time. Despite an extensive, months-long search,

I was left empty handed. At the urging of a friend, I applied to work for the city's parks and recreation department. I needed the money and figured it would be temporary at worst. I was hired within a matter of days. My shift began at 7:00 am and lasted until 3:30 in the afternoon. My responsibilities included picking up garbage, cleaning public toilets, mowing baseball diamonds, and blowing leaves.

Surprisingly, that sort of work was rather enjoyable. It was nice to not be in an intellectually demanding environment. Plus, I used my interactions with co-workers to talk about religion. I wanted to see if I could convert them to the Catholic faith.

Overall, that summer was a great experience, even if I didn't make a lot of money. Still, I didn't want to turn it into a career. I applied for more than thirty jobs elsewhere that fall and winter, mostly at Catholic schools and media companies. I had a few interviews, but nothing ever turned out.

"How is this my life?" I complained to a friend over beers one crisp spring afternoon. "I know people from college who have been working full-time making $45,000 a year since graduating five years ago. And here I am struggling to get by, handicapped by student loans and making less than $25,000. Didn't God say, in the Gospel of Matthew, that if we seek after Him everything will be given unto us? Well, where is *my* job? Where is *my* money? Where is *my* house, wife, and children?"

I returned to the parks job the ensuing year. It was literally the only place I could get hired. I felt like an utter failure. One summer is a nice break from reality. But two in a row?

On the first day of that second summer, mere minutes after punching in, I noticed a young man who looked familiar. I stood behind the shelves so as not to be seen. Within seconds, I remembered where I knew him. He'd taken the college success course I taught two years prior. In that class, I advised students on how to make smart career choices and how to find a company that appreciates their talents. Yet here I was, right alongside him picking up trash and cleaning toilets for a living. I couldn't have been more embarrassed.

The lesson in all this, I would only come to learn, was that God was humbling me, as one month later, a pro-life, Christian news organization called *LifeSiteNews* posted an online advertisement for a Digital Marketing Assistant. It was a work-from-home job that required email editing, headline writing, and a host of other social media skills I already had experience in.

After a series of interviews, I was offered the position. It was my first full-time "adult" job. I was thirty-one years old. I dropped to my knees when I received their offer. "The Lord hears the cries of the poor. Blessed be the Lord," I prayed. I quit the parks job the next day.

Humility Continued

In a letter written to women religious, St Alphonsus explains that there are a variety of other ways to practice humility, one of which is clothing choice. "Endeavor also to practice humility by the poverty of your furniture and of your garments," he urged them. "The dress of St Equitius was so humble, that, as St Gregory relates, they who had not known him would have scorned to salute him. Oh! what a source of edification is poverty of dress!"

In that same letter, he advised the women to shun self-praise and to refrain from ambition for worldly honors. He also encouraged them to not be disturbed by correction and to accept (and even be glad to receive) poor treatment from others. "The saints have not been made saints by applause and honor, but by injuries and insults," he wrote. St Alphonsus offers the following analogy on how we can practice humility in our own lives:

The chief occasion for practicing humility is when we are rebuked for some fault by superiors or others. Some people are like hedgehogs: when no one touches them, they seem quite placid and gentle; but no sooner does a Superior or a friend lay a hand on them, admonish them about something they have done badly, than they suddenly become all prickles, and bitingly reply that it is not true, or that they were right to act the way they did, or that such a correction is uncalled for. In a word, anyone who reproves them becomes their enemy; they behave like the people who accuse the surgeon for causing them pain while treating their wound.

Humility can also be practiced in our speech, St Alphonsus argues. A bombastic tongue, profane language, and babbling gossip are unbecoming of followers of Christ. "It is, according to St Ambrose, a violation of modesty to speak in a very loud tone," he writes. St Alphonsus shares the following remarks about why humility is essential to perfection:

> Humility is called a treasure because the Lord sees to it that the humble abound in good things. When a man's heart is full of himself, there is no room for God's gifts. Man must therefore ... be emptied of himself by the knowledge of his own nothingness.

To conclude this chapter, a summary of what has been said is in order. St Alphonsus teaches that we show our love for God by joyfully enduring the trials He sends us and by thanking Him, like Job did, for the good and bad things we experience. We grow in love of God first by desiring and then praying for it. We further advance in love of God when we humble ourselves, not only with our intellect, but in our actions, appearance, and in the manner in which we speak.

I'll now turn to the subject of prayer, which St Alphonsus teaches allows us to know God more closely and enables us to remain humble.

Considerations

- When I am sick, do I joyfully embrace my sufferings? When I am annoyed, do I complain? How can I apply to my own life the advice St Alphonsus has for those who want to show God they love Him?

- How can I be more like Job? Before going to bed tonight, what are four things that happened today I can thank God for?

- Of the five ways St Alphonsus says we can grow in love of God, which one resonates with me the most? Why? How can I put that into practice this week?

- St Thérèse of Lisieux told Jesus she wanted to be His "little plaything" and that she desired that He do whatever He wants with her. In what areas of my life can I adopt this attitude?

- What are some concrete ways I can acquire the virtue of humility? For instance, do I accept criticisms at work or from my religious superior with patience and resignation?

CHAPTER 3

PRAYER

Many spiritual writers have said that prayer is oxygen for the soul. St Alphonsus would have agreed with that. "If we leave off praying," he once wrote, "we shall be lost."

Why is prayer so important for St Alphonsus? Because "observance of the law, in the present state of our corrupt nature, is very difficult and even morally impossible without special assistance from God." He continues:

> Now, ordinarily speaking ... no Christian can be saved without ... asking for the graces necessary for his salvation. St Chrysostom says that as the soul is necessary for the life of the body, so is prayer necessary for the soul to preserve in the grace of God.

At its most basic level, prayer is the lifting of the soul to God. "Prayer, in a strict sense, says [St Thomas Aquinas], means recourse to God," St Alphonsus explains. "Prayer is an upward rising of the heart, it is a simple glance towards Heaven," says St Thérèse of Lisieux. Prayer "expands my heart and unites me to Jesus," she adds.[12] "True prayer is not in the sound of a voice," relates St Gregory the Great, "but in the desires of the heart."[13]

---

12 St Thérèse of Lisieux, *The Story of a Soul: A New Translation* (Brewster, MA: Paraclete Press, 2006), 274.
13 Bl. Columba Marmion, *Christ the Ideal of the Monk, Spiritual Conference*

Too often I encounter Catholics who don't really know how to pray. Sure, they know how to *recite* the Our Father, Hail Mary, and the Glory Be. But that's it. Rarely do they pray novenas, ask saints to intervene for them, say the Divine Office, go to adoration, or meditate. They seem to be wholly ignorant of how to communicate with God in different ways, so they end up turning to Protestantism, Buddhism, or some version of the erroneous "spiritual but not religious" mindset.

Like every good teacher, Christ Himself shows us how to pray. "And rising very early, going out, He went into a desert place: and there He prayed," Mark 1:35 states. "And having dismissed the multitude, He went into a mountain alone to pray," Matthew 14:23 says. "And He retired into the desert, and prayed," Luke 5:16 reads.

St Alphonsus says that in order to be united with God in prayer, we must "shut out all earthly attachments and inclinations." "When God desires to raise any soul to a high degree of perfection," he writes, "He inspires it to retire to some solitary place, far from the converse of creatures, and there He speaks to the ears, not of the body, but of the heart; and thus He enlightens and inflames it with His Divine Love."

St Alphonsus drives home this crucially important point by observing that when you first wake up in the morning your first thought should be of God and of "offering in His honor all that you will do or suffer in the course of the day." He also affirms that silence is essential for prayer:

> Silence is one of the principal means to attain the spirit of prayer and to form oneself for uninterrupted intercourse with God ... they who have the spirit of prayer love silence, which has deservedly been called a protector of innocence, a shield against temptations, and a fruitful source of prayer.

on the Monastic and Religious Life (St Louis, MO: B. Herder, 1926), 357.

Silence promotes recollection and awakens good thoughts in the heart. According to St Bernard, it forces the soul … to think of God and Heavenly things.

"It is hard to find a truly pious person who talks much," he adds.

Silence

Many people today seem to have an unhealthy fear of silence. According to one recent study, the average American checks their mobile device up to sixty-three times a day.[14] A 2020 survey of British adults found that individuals will spend nearly 34 years of their life looking at phones, laptops, and television sets.[15]

It goes without saying that in today's overly-connected world, computers and smart phones are required for almost every career. It's simply impossible to get away from them. At the same time, too many people can't put them down, even when the work day is over. It's as if they have a phobia of missing out on the latest news or trends. On this point, St Alphonsus explains that "the worldly shun solitude, and with good reason, for in solitude they feel more acutely the remorse of conscience." As such, "they go in search of the conversations and bustle of the world, that the noise of these occupations may stifle the stings of remorse."

But silence is precisely what allows God to communicate with us! "Speak, Lord, your servant is listening," the prophet Samuel said in the Old Testament.[16] I often wonder how souls can

---

14 Deyan Georgiev, "How Much Time Does the Average American Spend on Their Phone in 2023?" TechJury, 12 Jan 2023, https://techjury.net/blog/how-much-time-does-the-average-american-spend-on-their-phone/#gref.

15 Emma Elsworty, "Average adult will spend 34 years of their life looking at screens, poll claims," Independent, 22 May 2020, https://www.independent.co.uk/life-style/fashion/news/screen-time-average-lifetime-years-phone-laptop-tv-a9508751.html.

16 1 Samuel 3:10

grow in love of God when, mere minutes after waking up, they hop on their iPhones, turn on their radios, or listen to a podcast. How can they know what God wants from them if they begin their morning in this manner? Put another way, how can people have a relationship with God if they don't make time for Him at the start of their day, or at any time of the day for that matter? Answer: They can't! You cannot be friends with someone you don't talk to. "The more the heart is occupied with earthly concerns the less room there is in it for Divine Love," St Alphonsus teaches. "He who neglects to withdraw, at least now and then, from the thoughts of the world, and to retire to converse with God, has but little knowledge or light regarding the things of eternity." St Alphonsus would certainly be in a position to say such a thing, as he would often spend entire nights in silence before the Blessed Sacrament.

One of the first things I did after reading St Alphonsus' writings on prayer and silence was to turn off my car radio. Up until then, whenever I drove around town, I'd be listening to pop music or classic rock. The question wasn't whether the radio was going to be on. The question was, simply, how loud would it be?

As I came to a deeper understanding of the teachings of St Alphonsus, the less drawn I was to what the world considers music. Songs I once relied on to get me through the ups and downs of life no longer had the same consoling effect. I came to see them as nothing more than catchy forms of noise pollution that, if I happened to hear them, I frustratingly couldn't get out of my head for the next forty-eight hours. As St Alphonsus teaches, "Whosoever loves God, loves solitude. There the Lord communicates himself more familiarly to souls, because there He finds them less entangled in worldly affairs and more detached from earthly affections."

Eventually, I came to embrace the silence. If I drove somewhere, I would pray the Rosary. If I listened to anything, it was classical music or Gregorian chant. Think what you want, but that sort of music has an uplifting effect on the soul. Try it for a week and see what happens.

After I made these changes, I found myself freed from the obsession I had with the "entertainment" industry's latest up and coming "artists" and their mind-numbing, expletive-filled ballads. It was a truly liberating experience. I began to understand that I was experiencing what St Alphonsus calls the "solitude of the heart," which is what happens when we expel from the soul "every affection that is not for God."

A Traditional Catholic bishop once told me, "If our nature is warped, grace has nowhere to go. Christians should listen to Mozart and read Shakespeare if they want to dispose themselves to God's graces. And they should throw away those rotten smartphones and television sets. They're the devil's tabernacle!" He's absolutely right. And I believe St Alphonsus would agree with him.

A Lover of Music

Lest anyone think St Alphonsus was opposed to music of any kind, it must be made known that he himself was a sort of prodigy, spending—at his father's command—hours on end studying it in his youth. As a result, by the age of twelve he was considered something of a master harpsichordist.

Although later in life he regretted the time he spent with music in his youth, St Alphonsus used his talents to compose spiritual hymns and poems to enhance his missionary efforts. One of his most popular melodies is From Starry Skies Thou Comest (*"Tu Scendi dalle Stelle"*), a Christmas carol he composed as a young priest in 1732. It is regarded, even to this day, as one of the most famous Italian songs ever created. In total, he crafted

about fifty hymns. One of them on the love the soul has for
Christ is presented below:

> World, thou art no more for me;
> World, I am no more for thee;
> All affection, dear or sweet,
> All are laid at Jesus' feet.
>
> He has so enamored me
> Of his heavenly charity,
> That no earthly goods inspire
> Aught of love or vain desire.
>
> Jesus, Love, be Thou my own;
> Thee I long for—Thee alone;
> All myself I give to Thee,
> Do what'er Thou wilt with me.
>
> Life without Thy love would be
> Death, O Sovereign Good! to me.
> Bound and held by Thy dear chains,
> Captive now my heart remains.
>
> O my Life! my soul from Thee
> Can henceforth no longer flee;
> By thy loving arrows slain,
> Now Thy prey it must remain.
>
> If ungrateful worms like me
> Merit not the love of Thee,
> Thou, sweet Lord, hast well deserved
> To be ever loved and served.
>
> Then, O God, my heart inflame;
> Give that love which Thou dost claim;
> Payment I will ask for none,
> Love demands but love alone.

God of Beauty, Lord of Light!
Thy good will is my delight;
Now henceforth Thy will divine
Ever shall in all be mine.

Come, O Jesus, I implore,
Pierce my heart, 'tis mine no more;
Kindle in my breast Thy fire,
That of love I may expire.

Ah! my Spouse, I love but Thee;
Thou my Love shalt ever be,
Thee I love; I love and sigh
For Thy love one day to die.

Alphonsus' compositions greatly aided in his already successful efforts to spread the Catholic faith. They also combatted
blasphemous language, which he personally despised. "Music is
an art which must be practiced in its perfection—otherwise, it
does not produce pleasure, but disgust," he once remarked.

A Foretaste of Heaven?

Another turning point in my spiritual journey came when I was
thirty-two years old. I was contemplating whether I should apply
to the seminary, so I decided to attend a five-day Ignatian retreat
in Connecticut. The only thing was that it was a silent retreat.
What that means is that for five days straight you're not allowed
to speak to any of the other retreatants. You're only allowed to
talk to the priests.

As an introvert, I relished the silence. I spent the bulk of the
week praying in my room, walking the property, and reflecting
on Psalm 46: "Be still and know that I am the Lord."

Two days into the retreat, the electricity went out thanks to a thunderstorm that rolled through the area. The two dozen young men in attendance and I were forced to sit by candlelight as priests gave lectures about spiritual combat and how the devil wants to drag us to hell. It was downright medieval.

Eventually, God rewarded me on the last day with an intense mystical experience when we were praying the Rosary in the chapel as a group. We had just started the second Glorious Mystery, the Ascension of Christ into Heaven. My eyes were fixed on the statue of Mary in front of me. Suddenly, I was overtaken by a contemplation so powerful that my surroundings began to seem transparent. It wasn't an out of body experience, but it felt as if the universe opened up to me in a transcendent manner, like my soul was in touch with reality outside of time and space.

I later told my friends that in the two minutes or so that I had that feeling, it was as if the pews and walls in the chapel had no material essence to them. It was like the layers of this world were peeled away and I was transported to a purely spiritual state of being that enabled me to fully grasp, just for a moment, how empty and passing this world really is.

Why God decided to give me that great gift is something only He can answer. I imagine it's because He wanted to show me that everything in this life is vanity and that when I encounter sufferings and temptations later on, I'll cling to that moment in order to remain faithful to Him. Whether I'm right or wrong about that, those precious seconds are something I've never forgotten. I look forward to remembering them on my deathbed to help me through my final trials.

To Enter Under Our Roof

It should be obvious why St Alphonsus so strongly recommends silence for those who are striving to be perfect. "Silence promotes recollection and awakens good thoughts in the heart," he teaches.

The simple yet sad fact is that persons mired in sin don't know how to be silent. They prefer the noise of the world because the absence of sound forces them to confront reality as it is. "Worldly-minded people shun solitude ... for it is in retirement that they are troubled with the qualms of conscience," St Alphonsus points out. Television and other distractions keep our gaze fixed on this side of eternity, instead of on Heaven where it should be. On this point, St Alphonsus says the following:

> In prayer we conceive holy thoughts, we practice devout affections, we excite great desires, and form efficacious resolutions to give ourselves wholly to God; and thus the soul is led ... to sacrifice earthly pleasures and all disorderly appetites.

At the end of the day, we can't hear what God is trying to say to us if our attention is elsewhere. We can't keep locking Him out of our lives. We have to give Him a chance, like the Roman centurion said, to "enter under our roof."[17] Silent retreats, turning off car radios, and putting away our mobile devices are perfect opportunities for doing just that.

Types of Prayer

How should Christians pray? And what should they pray for? The Church Fathers are unanimous in saying there are four types of prayer: thanksgiving, petition, contrition, and adoration.

A prayer of thanksgiving, St Alphonsus observes, is "returning of thanks for benefits received." A prayer of petition is asking God for a particular favor. A prayer of contrition is to beg

17 Matthew 8:8

for God's pardon. A prayer of adoration is a prayer offered in praise of God.

In his many writings, St Alphonsus makes special mention of several different methods of prayer: vocal prayer, ejaculatory prayer, and mental or "meditative" prayer. I'd like to take a moment to explain each of these.

Vocal prayer is "very pleasing to God because by it the endless Majesty of God is glorified and acknowledged," he writes. But vocal prayer, so that it "may tend to God's glory and our own salvation ... must be accompanied by attention and devotion." St Alphonsus, referencing the words of St Gregory, clarifies his remarks by adding:

> If we wish ... to please God we must pray not only with the lips, but also with the heart.... [A]ttention is directed to the words when you are careful to pronounce them well; it is directed to the sense of the words when you try to understand their meaning.

The devil, he continues, is "intent upon turning our thoughts toward worldly affairs during prayer."

St Alphonsus contends that the easiest means of practicing vocal prayer consists in uttering fervent ejaculations. What is an ejaculatory prayer? Ejaculatory prayers are "pious outpourings of the heart" that "need not be restricted to any particular place or time. They are in order at all times and in all places at work, at meals, at recreation, at home or away from home," he further observes. "Among all the ejaculations and prayers, the invocation of holy names of Jesus, Mary and Joseph should have the first place."

More than anything, ejaculatory prayers are spontaneous bursts of love directed toward God. One example of an ejaculatory prayer might be, "Jesus, banish from my soul thoughts of impurity and evil!" Another could be, "O my God, allow me to get through this workday with charity and patience, and to treat my co-workers with love." One ejaculatory prayer that I found particularly helpful during a retreat I made in Ireland not long ago is the following:

> My King and My Queen, make me Thy slave. Take my heart and my mind. Make my hands, my feet, and my entire body Yours alone. Possess me, O Lord, for Thou hast created me. You have rights over everything I am. Mary, my mother, help me know and serve Our King and thee all the days of my life. Amen.

St Alphonsus also recommends that Catholics engage in meditative or "mental" prayer. "Without mental prayer, the soul is without light," he teaches. "The eternal truths are spiritual things; they cannot be seen with the bodily eyes, but only with the eyes of the soul, that is to say, by reflection and meditation." St Alphonsus says the following on how to engage in mental prayer:

> In order to practice … meditation, and to make it truly profitable to the soul, we must well ascertain the ends for which we attempt it. We must meditate in order to unite ourselves more completely to God. It is not so much good thoughts in the intellect as good acts of the will, or holy desires, that unite us to God; and such are the acts that we perform in meditation—acts of humility, confidence, self-sacrifice, resignation, and especially of love and of repentance for our sins.

"Without meditation," St Alphonsus continues, we will not have the "strength to resist the temptations of our enemies, and to practice the virtues of the Gospel."

At the end of the day, we should approach prayer as if we were speaking to God "as a dear friend," he teaches.

St Veronica, Pray for Me

When I first started meditating, it didn't come naturally. Not only would I get distracted after only a couple minutes, I didn't really get anything out of it. The problem, it turns out, was that I had been so used to repetitive vocal prayers (the Our Father, the Hail Mary, etc.) that meditation was a completely foreign exercise to me. I was a total rookie whose meditation "muscles" were in a state of atrophy. A breakthrough came when I meditated on St Veronica.

Most Catholics are aware that St Veronica wiped the face of Christ as He made His way to Calvary. The garment Christ imprinted His face on, also known as the Veil of Veronica, is housed in St Peter's Basilica in Rome and is venerated by the Church. There's even a "Holy Face of Jesus" novena Catholics can pray.

I always had a certain fascination with St Veronica, even in my youth. Here she was, this gentle woman in the midst of a chaotic, dangerous environment where passions were running high. Yet, instead of sitting on the sidelines and being an indifferent bystander, her love for God moved her to action, so much so that she risked her own safety in order to alleviate Christ's sufferings.

One summer night about four years ago, I was at the local adoration chapel. I couldn't decide what to meditate on. I was thumbing through the Bible, but nothing stood out. I then came across Christ's Passion. I instantly thought about St Veronica.

"Okay Lord. I have not been meditating well at all lately. I really need your help tonight. Can you help me make a good meditation? St Veronica, can you help me? Can you pray for me? Let me understand whatever it is you want me to know as I reflect on your love for Christ. I beg thee, open my heart to God's Will so I can grow in perfection."

I began to picture in my head what the road to Calvary looked like. First, I thought about the different persons involved—impatient Roman soldiers shouting at Jesus to "hurry it up!" Irate Jews cursing at Him and calling Our Lord terrible names. I then imagined what was actually taking place—Christ falling to the ground multiple times. Women crying over His pain. I then saw St Veronica and how she likely would have been a rather small woman. I began to think about how she had to muster up the courage to find her way to Jesus through the unruly crowd. I thought of how wiping Christ's face (though not as immense a gift as Simon carrying His actual cross) was a great work of mercy, as it was the most she could possibly offer.

"Veronica, you who were so moved by compassion," I began to pray, "inspire me to also act with courage and love of Our Lord and to not shy away from doing what I am capable of in this life. Pray that I may be granted the humility to not be jealous of those who can do more than me. Enable me to use the talents God has given me to the fullest and to be content with the results I obtain. Ask our Heavenly Father to bestow upon me an awareness of knowing when and how to put myself into situations where there is a great need for me. Help me to not give in to peer pressure. Inspire me to take action, like you did, even though the enemies of Christ may persecute me for doing so, so that I can also help Jesus accomplish His Divine Plan. St Veronica, pray for me."

I left the chapel that evening not only on the receiving end of a tremendous consolation, but in possession of a much richer understanding of this beautiful yet overlooked saint. I also came to better grasp the virtues she possessed and the unique role she played in the Passion of Our Lord. I went to bed more confident in how to meditate and what to meditate on in order to grow closer to God. I hope that St Veronica is a saint you will pray to as well.

General Rules for Praying

Before we pray, St Alphonsus says we should follow some basic ground rules so it will be beneficial.

First, he advises that we "dismiss all distracting thoughts and say what St Bernard said on entering a church: 'Remain here, all you earthly and distracting thoughts. I may have leisure for you after meditation.'"

St Alphonsus also instructs us to say, out loud, an act of faith and to beg God's mercy while imploring Him to hear our prayer. "During prayer, avoid haste," he teaches. "Many people, when praying, seem to be intent on reaching the end of prayers, as if it were a torture that must be endured, but during the shortest possible time. Such irreverent haste can hardly be pleasing to God or profitable to us."

There are other tips St Alphonsus provides to those who want to pray well. When you meditate, "ask pardon for your past offenses, and beg for light and grace to make your meditation well," he says. "Recommend yourself to the Blessed Virgin, St Joseph, your Guardian Angel and your holy patrons." Use a book, he adds. "Pause from time to time when you are particularly impressed in order that, like the bee, you may extract the honey from the flower."

When we finish praying, we should thank God for hearing us and make a firm determination to carry out the resolutions we made. We should also ask God to help us stay close to Him and to have mercy on the holy souls in purgatory.

Unanswered Prayers

Everyone has prayers that go unanswered. But that's not because God doesn't hear them. Scripture tells us He does. "And this is the confidence that we have toward Him, that if we ask anything according to His Will He hears us," 1 John 5:14 says. If we aren't getting what we want when we pray, it's likely that we are praying for things that God, in His inscrutable wisdom, has decided aren't good for us.

When I was experiencing my neurological symptoms in my early thirties, I feverishly went from one hospital to the next, spending tens of thousands of dollars on various scans and tests. But none of them provided an explanation for what was happening. At night, I cried myself to sleep. "Heal me, Lord! Hear the cries of your servant! My Jesus, mercy! I can't take this anymore!"

I began invoking every saint I knew to pray for me. I did multiple novenas to St Thérèse and to the Sacred Heart of Jesus as well. When those prayers weren't answered, I got angry. Furious, even. Spiritually, I was a mess. I spent most of my evenings focusing on my symptoms. I even fell into the trap of telling myself how "pointless" life was. One evening while with a friend, I murmured, "If God made us to suffer, why did He even create man in the first place? For fun just to watch us writhe about in agony? What a joke!"

Despite my frustration, I started visiting the local cemetery three to four times a week to pray for the dead. In return, I asked them to intercede for me by begging God that I'd be cured, or, at the very least, that I would find out what this illness was in the first place. At night, I visited the Blessed Sacrament at the nearby adoration chapel, repeating the penitential Psalms—especially Psalm 6—over and over: "Rebuke me not in thy indignation, O Lord, nor chastise me in thy wrath. Have mercy on me, O Lord, for I am weak: heal me, Lord, for my bones are troubled."

Despite constantly praying and making dozens of trips to not only the chapel but also to the YMCA (I lost seventy pounds over a period of ten months), I wasn't improving. I eventually came to grips with the fact that this ailment wasn't going anywhere, and that maybe that is what God wanted for me and that His silence in the face of my prayers was in fact His answer *to* my prayers.

I began to realize that He wanted me to patiently endure my illness to prove to Him that I would trust Him. I started embracing my symptoms with as much joy as I could, offering them up for my past offenses, for the conversion of wayward clergy, for my future spouse or religious vocation, and for my friends and family.

I eventually did get some answers to my prayers soon after that. I'd been seeing several naturopathic doctors and was advised to go on a strict detox diet to heal what was found to be a "fatty liver." I was also told I had small intestine bacteria overgrowth, also known as SIBO. This was apparently causing digestive issues that were impacting my neurological system elsewhere in my body. It was by no means an easy process, but I was able to rid myself of some of my symptoms by disciplining my appetite and adopting an even more rigorous workout routine.

The moral of the story is this: we have to pray and trust in God, even if we don't get the outcomes we desire. God is the physician of our soul, not merely the doctor of our bodies. How could He, being all-loving, prescribe us something that would endanger our eternal well-being? He knows what's best for us. We do not. "Oh, the depth of the riches of the wisdom and of the knowledge of God! How incomprehensible are His judgments, and how unsearchable His ways!" Romans 11:33 reminds us. We simply have to throw ourselves before God's Wisdom if we want to be perfect like our Father in Heaven.

Praying Well

Before moving on to Chapter 4 and discussing what St Alphonsus teaches about Holy Communion, it's important to point out what he says about praying well:

The Lord does indeed regard the prayers of His servants, but only of His servants who are humble.... He does not hear the prayers of the proud who trust in their own strength; but for that reason leaves them to their own feebleness.

Our prayers must also be confident. "If we wish by prayer to obtain grace from God ... we [should] pray with a confidence that feels sure of being heard," St Alphonsus adds, referencing St James. He goes on:

When we cease from prayer, when we stop conversing with God, we allow ourselves to focus on earthly matters. Satan goes about like a roaring lion. We must ever be on guard and seeking to grow closer to God. Just like the poor men who outside of Jerusalem continued to beg for alms, we too must incessantly ask God, daily, for help.

As already mentioned, we have to pray for that which will truly help our souls. God loves to shower us with gifts. But if we're asking Him to let us win the lottery, chances are that prayer won't be answered. "But," you might say, "if I had all of that money I could help a lot of people." Do you know that for sure? Maybe you'd end up squandering it on material possessions. Maybe you'd be consumed with it and would turn it into an idol. Or maybe it would divide your family. There are plenty of horror stories about lottery winners who ended up bankrupt, divorced, or worse, murdered. God is infinitely wiser than we are. He knows us far better than we know ourselves. It's better to trust Him than to think He's not acting lovingly towards us because our prayers aren't answered in the time or manner we want.

If we continually find our prayers aren't being answered, we can conclude several things, St Alphonsus says. One is that we're not beseeching God humbly. Two is that we're not praying as often as we should. Three is that we might be praying for the wrong things. And four, we're not placing enough trust in God.

If we find ourselves doing these and we're still not obtaining what we want, God might just want to see if we're going to persevere until the end. "Delay is not denial," my grandma used to say. "Just because something doesn't happen when we want it to doesn't mean it won't ever happen."

We can also ask the saints or the Blessed Virgin Mary to intercede for us. Many things that are asked from God, St Alphonsus writes, are asked from Mary, and are obtained. This is because God loves to honor His Mother.

If, however, none of these methods are effective, and our requests are still left wanting, our only option is to repeat the words Our Lord said to the prophet Isaiah: "For My thoughts are not your thoughts, neither are your ways My ways."[18]

It's important to recall that our trust in God is tested not in times of riches and abundance but in times of adversity. Look at St Peter when he walked on water with Our Lord. He wouldn't have had any worries if it was a nice summer day and the lake was calm. Instead, he was tried in the middle of a storm. When his faith failed him, he began to sink. But Jesus was there in the end to preserve his life. Similarly, God sometimes tests us by allowing the chaos in our lives to rage on. He does this for our greater good. God surely loves the humble heart and always hears the prayers of those who seek Him. He will help us—but on His time.

Considerations

- How often do I pray? Am I praying consistently, and with confidence and humility? Or do I only pray once in a while and stop when my requests are unanswered? What changes to my prayer life can I make based on St Alphonsus' recommendations?

18 Isaiah 55:8

- How many hours did I spend with my phone, computer, or other electronic devices today? How many did I spend with God? Where in my schedule can I find more time to be alone with Him?

- Are the television shows, forms of entertainment, and music I listen to helping my prayer life or hindering it? Can I go one week (or even one day) without them? Is silence difficult for me? What would St Alphonsus say to me if he were alive today and I had to tell him my answers to these questions?

- When was the last time I went on a retreat, did a novena, said an ejaculatory prayer, or meditated? What are some different ways I can pray this month that I haven't before?

- Who is my favorite saint and why? How can I get to know them better so I can imitate their virtues even more? Which three saints can I meditate on and grow closer to in the next three months?

CHAPTER 4

THE BLESSED SACRAMENT

"There is no way we can be more perfectly united with Jesus than receiving Him in Communion," St Alphonsus teaches. "There is nothing more agreeable to God than for us to receive Holy Communion."

But if the last sixty or so years have shown us anything, it's that fewer and fewer Catholics are receiving Communion as they should. As a result, they're not obtaining the spiritual benefits God wants to give them.

In 2019, Pew Research released a shocking study that discovered seven in ten Catholics in the United States don't believe Our Lord is substantially present in the Eucharist at Mass. They said that the bread and wine are mere "symbols."[19] Astonishingly, forty-three percent who thought that believed that's actually what the Church teaches. Others were just ignorant of Catholic doctrine.

What's more, a study published by Gallup in 2018 found that only thirty-nine percent of Catholics attend Mass on a weekly basis. Those numbers only get worse based on age, with a paltry twenty-five percent of Catholics in their twenties attending

---

19 Gregory Smith, "Just one-third of U.S. Catholics agree with their church that Eucharist is body, blood of Christ," Pew Research Center, 5 Aug 2019, https://www.pewresearch.org/fact-tank/2019/08/05/transubstantiation-eucharist-u-s-catholics/.

weekly Mass. For comparison's sake, weekly Mass attendance in 1955 (before the Second Vatican Council) was around seventy-five percent.[20]

These sad statistics easily explain why so many Catholics disagree with the Church's infallible teachings on homosexual "marriage," abortion, pre-marital sex, contraception, and other issues related to family life.[21] I often tell friends of mine, "If only these poor souls understood what the Eucharist is, and only if priests taught the hard truths of our faith, maybe Catholics would wake up to the lies they're being told by the world about sexuality."

According to St Alphonsus, there is nothing more beneficial for a soul than Holy Communion. But in order for Catholics to receive its benefits, they need to do two things. First, they need to be in the right spiritual state. They need, in other words, to properly prepare for Communion. Second, they need to thank God afterwards. "It is certain that the saints derived great profit from their Communions," St Alphonsus writes, but "only because they were careful to prepare themselves well for receiving" it.

How, then, can Catholics prepare to receive Our Lord at Mass? The first thing they should do, St Alphonsus says, is to disengage their heart from everything that is not God. "The more the heart is occupied with Earthly concerns, the less room there is in it for Divine Love." The second thing they should do is have an actual "desire" to receive Christ so they can "advance in His love." We can't, in other words, go to Mass with the primary intention of keeping up appearances with our neighbors, or catching up on the latest gossip and hanging out with friends afterward. What we're really at Mass for is to worship and unite ourselves to God.

20 Lydia Saad, "Catholics' Church Attendance Resumes Downward Slide," Gallup, 9 Apr 2018, https://news.gallup.com/poll/232226/church-attendance-among-catholics-resumes-downward-slide.aspx

21 Dalia Fahmy, "8 key findings about Catholics and abortion," Pew Research Center, 20 Oct 2020, https://www.pewresearch.org/fact-tank/2020/10/20/8-key-findings-about-catholics-and-abortion/.

St Alphonsus further recommends that Catholics mortify their senses and passions during their daily lives in order to remain free from sin and prepare for Holy Communion. Catholics should also make a half hour of mental prayer every morning. I'm sure if he were alive today, he'd also instruct Catholics to abstain from social media before Mass and to refrain from talking about worldly topics (or listening to the radio) on the drive to church as well.

Growing Closer to God

As was just mentioned, thanking God after receiving the Holy Eucharist is essential if we want to advance in perfection. "After Communion, we are, says St Chrysostom, one body and one flesh with Jesus Christ," St Alphonsus recalls.

He further advises that we put ourselves in deep communication with God, and not, as so many Catholics seem to do today, look around at others and whisper to their neighbor. "Oh! What great graces are lost by those who spend but little time in prayer after Communion," he laments. He continues:

> The prayer we make after Communion is the most acceptable to God, and the most profitable to us. After Communion the soul should be employed in affections and petitions. The affections ought to consist not only in acts of thanksgiving, but also in acts of humility, of love, and of oblation of ourselves to God. Let us then humble ourselves as much as possible at the sight of a God made our food after we had offended Him.

St Alphonsus further adds: "We should not only make these affectations, but we ought also to present to God with great confidence many petitions for His graces. The time after Communion is a time in which we can gain treasures of divine graces."

If Catholics today don't believe that the Eucharist is the actual Body, Blood, Soul, and Divinity of Our Lord and Savior Jesus Christ, there is no way they can draw spiritual benefits from it. How sad this must make God, who desires so much to be united with us in this life and in the next.

An Increase in Love and Patience

When I came back to the Catholic faith, it was the Traditional Latin Mass that really got me hooked. I'd been attending the *Novus Ordo* liturgy (the one created after Vatican II in the 1960s) in the years prior on a semi-regular basis. But if I'm being honest, my spiritual life was stuck in second gear. I wasn't going to confession regularly and I certainly wasn't following St Alphonsus' advice on preparing for and giving thanks after Communion.

Whenever I went to the modern Mass growing up, it always felt like a social event. The contemporary music, the holding of hands during the Our Father, and the constant responses to the priest's words never really made me feel closer to God. Far from being something sacred, the liturgy felt more like a theatrical play where the priest—and not God—was the center of attention. On top of that, I was wholly irritated by the way some clergy walked up and down the center aisle during their sermon as if the Mass was some sort of neighborhood block party. Recent studies do suggest that young Catholics share at least some of these concerns, as they are attending in great numbers and with more regularity the older liturgy.[22] [23] [24]

22 Virginia Aabram, "3 Reasons Why the Latin Mass Is So Attractive to Young People," National Catholic Register, 23 Aug 2021, https://www.ncregister.com/blog/3-reasons-why-young-catholics-love-latin-mass.

23 "The Growth of the Latin Mass: A Survey," Crisis Magazine, 26 Jul 2021, https://www.crisismagazine.com/opinion/the-growth-of-the-latin-mass-a-survey.

24 "The Latin Mass Among Millennials & Gen Z: A National Study," Priestly

I distinctly remember the first time I went to the Traditional Latin Mass. I especially recall the silence. No one was chit-chatting. No one was mulling about. Everyone was kneeling and praying the Rosary. All the women had veils on and were wearing skirts. God was clearly the focal point of everything.

During Mass, it was as if time stood still. I wasn't worried about how long it lasted like I had been with the *Novus Ordo*. Furthermore, the moment of consecration was clearly the apex of the liturgy, and not the sermon or the exchange of peace, as the Masses I attended growing up made them seem to be. Everything about it reflected the true essence of the Catholic faith: hierarchical, sacrificial, Christo-centric, and reverential. To say the very least, attending the Latin Mass has been a game-changer for my spiritual life.

Catholics living in the United States usually rely on an English-language missal when attending the Latin Mass so they can understand what is going on. I acquired mine from my then seventy-eight year-old grandmother. Inside the missal was a prayer written by St Thomas Aquinas on thanking God after receiving Communion. That prayer, presented below, should be, in my opinion, recited by all Catholics. It's served me well in my own spiritual life and fulfills, in every way, St Alphonsus' recommendation that we give thanks to God after receiving the Eucharist.

I thank Thee, O holy Lord, almighty Father, eternal God, Who have deigned, not through any merits of mine, but out of the condescension of Thy goodness, to satisfy me a sinner, Thy unworthy servant, with the precious Body and Blood of Thy Son, our Lord Jesus Christ. I pray that this Holy Communion be not a condemnation to punishment for me, but a saving plea to forgiveness. May it be to me

Fraternity of St Peter, 5 Jun 2020 https://fssp.com/latin-mass-among-millennials-study/.

the armor of faith and the shield of a good will. May it be the emptying out of my vices and the extinction of all lustful desires; an increase of charity and patience, of humility and obedience, and of all virtues; a strong defense against the snares of all my enemies, visible and invisible; the perfect quieting of all my evil impulses of flesh and spirit, binding me firmly to Thee, the one true God; and a happy ending of my life. I pray too that Thou will deign to bring me a sinner to that ineffable banquet, where Thou with Thy Son and the Holy Spirit, are to Your saints true light, fulfillment of desires, eternal joy, unalloyed gladness, and perfect bliss. Through the same Christ our Lord. Amen.

Drinking Judgment

Preparing for Mass is just as important as thanking God after receiving Communion. Unsurprisingly, St Thomas composed a prayer for that as well, to be said before Mass begins. It, too, was in my grandma's missal and is presented here:

Almighty and everlasting God, I approach the sacrament of Thy Only begotten Son, our Lord Jesus Christ. As a sick man I approach the physician of life; as a man unclean, I come to the fountain of mercy; blind, to the light of eternal brightness; poor and needy, to the Lord of Heaven and earth. I beseech Thee, therefore, in Thy boundless mercy, to heal my sickness, to wash away my defilements, to enlighten my blindness, to enrich my poverty, and to clothe my nakedness; that I may receive the Bread of angels, the King of kings, the Lord of lords, with such reverence and humility, such contrition and faith, such purpose and intention, as may help the salvation of my soul. Grant, I beseech Thee, that I may receive not only the Sacrament of the Body and Blood of our Lord, but also the whole grace and virtue of the Sacrament. O most indulgent God, grant me so to receive the Body of Thy Only begotten Son, our Lord Jesus Christ, which He took of the Virgin Mary, that I may be found worthy to be incorporated with His Mystical Body and numbered among His members. O most loving Father, grant that I may one day forever contemplate Him unveiled and face to face, Whom, on my pilgrimage, I receive under a veil, Thy beloved Son, who with Thee lives and reigns in the unity of the Holy Spirit, God, world without end. Amen.

Preparing for Holy Communion is not just something St Thomas and St Alphonsus recommend. Scripture advises us to do that as well. "Those who eat and drink without discerning the body of Christ eat and drink judgment on themselves," 1 Corinthians 11:29 states. What this means is that if we approach the Eucharist in a state of sin, we're actually committing another sin by receiving it. To use an analogy, when we receive God in Communion when we're not in a state of grace, we're essentially inviting Him into a torture chamber filled with polluted air.

At the end of the day, the best way to follow St Alphonsus' advice on preparing for Holy Communion is to confess our sins to a priest and to promise God we will avoid all occasions of sin in the future. "The Holy Ghost tells us ... we must fly from sin as from a serpent," he writes. "No, says St Cyprian; it is impossible to stand in the midst of flames, and not be burned," he adds.

St Joseph, a Humble Leader

One saint that laity—but especially priests—should pray to more often is St Joseph. Not only is he considered the "Terror of Demons" and protector of the Church, he was, during his earthly life, the foster father of Our Lord, a role that allowed Him to have the most intimate relationship a created man could ever have with Jesus. Who better for us to turn to, aside from the Blessed Virgin Mary herself, in order to prepare ourselves to be united with Christ in Holy Communion?

I myself began a relationship with St Joseph during a visit to adoration in my mid-thirties. I never really knew what adoration was until my junior year of college. I'm sure I was taught about its importance at some point in my youth—having gone to a Catholic grade school and high school—but I don't recall being encouraged to practice it.

A female friend of mine named Erin introduced me to adoration when I was an undergraduate. We were partners leading a group of students for freshman orientation at the small, Catholic liberal arts school we attended in West Michigan. We grew closer in the ensuing years and she asked me one wintry evening if I wanted to go to the chapel down the road. Despite not having a clue as to what it would be like (although I was curious) I agreed to tag along.

"What, you just sit here?" I whispered after we entered.

"Talk to Jesus," she quipped. "Read the Bible. Just drink in the goodness of the Lord."

"How am I supposed to do that?" I thought to myself as I tried to take my seat as naturally as possible so the five people in the room wouldn't suspect I was wholly ignorant about what I was doing.

The best I can remember from that particular night is that I just stared at the Eucharist in silence. It was the silence that was the most memorable part of the visit. The world just stopped and my focus was on God alone. I'd never experienced something like that before.

It took another eight years for me to fully embrace adoration on a regular basis. At that point, I was visiting anywhere from three to five times a week, usually from 10 pm to 11 pm. I'd often go, sit, and pray Compline or meditate on the Psalms. Other times, I read the Gospel. I spent several New Year's Eve's there as the clock struck midnight.

One of the most powerful moments I had during my reversion came at adoration while meditating on St Joseph. My visit began by asking God to clear my mind and to help me get out of it whatever He wanted me to. I closed my eyes and flipped through the Bible. My finger landed on Matthew 2:13, the flight of the Holy Family into Egypt. I began to picture in my head St Joseph and the Blessed Mother traveling through the hot desert.

"Was he nervous? What was he thinking at the time?" I pondered. "Could I do that for my spouse if God asked me to? Will I have the courage to lead a family or parish one day? Lord, help me be like St Joseph. Lord, let me be as faithful to you as he was."

After reflecting on St Joseph for a little while longer, I began to realize how humble yet how masculine he really was. I came to view him as a spiritual guide and as a holy guardian. I also considered how he could have cashed in on Jesus' fame, and how he could have charged admission to Jews who wanted a "sneak peek" at "the Savior of Mankind's birthplace." He literally could have made it a tourist attraction and published a memoir about his life. Instead, he submitted to God's plan and remained a simple laborer, a diligent father, and a loving husband, directing Mary and Jesus with strength and fortitude every day. All of this made me appreciate St Joseph more than I did before. Unlike the phony machismo that many social media influencers peddle to young men seeking meaning in today's effeminate society, St Joseph is the personification of real masculinity in that he lived a life of virtue and sacrifice for others. I often ask him to make me a better (and holier) man. I pray you will too.

I Am With You Always

The level of dedication professional athletes have for their craft is legendary. During their careers, many Hall of Fame basketball players visited the gym multiple times a day. Top golfers spend hours on end at the driving range before tournaments so they won't miscalculate even one shot. NFL quarterbacks consult their trainers during the off season in order to remain in peak physical shape so they can lead their team to victory.

What a shame it is to see Catholics not taking the same approach to their spiritual lives, and instead of doing novenas, performing works of mercy, and visiting the closest adoration chapel, they indulge in worldly entertainments, leave off praying, and stop communicating with God altogether. "The person who loves Jesus lives in His company," St Alphonsus reminds us. "Souls inflamed with the love of God loved to dwell in the presence of the Most Holy Sacrament."

One of the first things St Alphonsus did after taking up residence in the Diocese of St Agatha of the Goths was to open his church to the public so they could adore the Blessed Sacrament with him. As previously mentioned, St Alphonsus loved spending time in front of the Eucharist. But he also knew that the main purpose of adoration is not the consolations we sometimes receive from it. "We ought not go into prayer simply in order to taste the sweetness of Divine Love," he remarks. "It would be a waste of time to go for such a reason and it will bring us scant profit. We should give time to prayer simply to please God, or in other words, to discover what God wants from us and to ask His help in carrying it out."

The theology St Alphonsus relies on to explain why Our Lord remained on earth in the form of bread after His ascension is marvelous, and is worth presenting here:

Our loving Shepherd, who has given His life for us who are His sheep, would not separate Himself from us by death. 'My beloved sheep,' He says, 'I am always with you. It is for you I have remained on earth in this Sacrament; here you find Me whenever you wish, ready to help and console you by My presence.'

St Alphonsus further explains:

At the bidding of a man, the King of Heaven comes down onto the altar, and He dwells there ... He allows Himself to be carried wherever men take Him, whether it be into houses or through the public streets. He allows himself to be given in Holy Communion to anyone who comes to receive Him, whether he be in the state of grace or in mortal sin. St Luke tells us that while He lived on earth He obeyed Our Lady and St Joseph. In the Blessed Sacrament, He obeys as many men as there are priests in the world.

Can You Not Spend One Hour With Me?

In his writings on adoration, St Alphonsus encourages Catholics to spend time in front of Our Lord every day. "You will probably gain more by praying fifteen minutes before the Blessed Sacrament than by all other spiritual exercises of the day."

He also teaches that "amongst all devotions, after that of receiving the Sacraments, that of adoring Jesus in the Blessed Sacrament holds first place, is the most pleasing to God, and the most useful to ourselves." For what purpose "did Jesus remain on earth in this Sacrament?" he also asks. "He remains there because He cannot bear to separate Himself from us, as He has said that He takes a delight in us."

The real beauty of adoration is that it really is Christ right in front of you. How many presidents or governors would give you the time of day to shake your hand and hear your concerns? Typically, you have to make a major campaign donation just to get a photograph with them. But adoration is free of charge. And the Lord of the universe is there to hear whatever you want to say, for however long you want to say it. What a loving God we have! St Alphonsus knew this all too well.

> It is not permitted in the world for persons of all ranks to speak alone with kings; but with Jesus Christ, the King of kings, both nobles and plebeians, rich and poor, can converse at their will, setting before Him their wants, and seeking His grace; and there Jesus gives audiences to all, hears all, and comforts all.

"The kings of the earth," St Alphonsus also says, "give audiences a few times in the year, but God gives a continual audience."

These remarks should make it obvious why the late Bishop Fulton J. Sheen (1895–1979) spoke so highly about adoration. In his autobiography, he wrote, "The only time our Lord asked the Apostles for anything was the night He went into agony.... Not for an hour of activity did He plead, but for an hour of companionship."[25]

We should heed this advice and visit adoration chapels as frequently as possible, always remembering to venerate the Blessed Sacrament as much as we can during our brief lives. As St Alphonsus says, "Christ especially delights in the meditation that is made before the Blessed Sacrament, since there it appears that He bestows light and grace most abundantly upon those who visit Him."

---

25 Ven. Fulton Sheen, *Treasure in Clay: The Autobiography of Fulton J. Sheen* (Image Books/Doubleday, 2008), 197–198.

Christ, Our True Soulmate

It's not uncommon to hear Catholics say that they are unable to visit the Blessed Sacrament. "The chapel is too far away." "I have children to take care of." "I haven't bought groceries for the week yet." "I don't get anything out of it."

Some of these are not wholly unreasonable excuses. A mother of five cannot be faulted for prioritizing her children's temporal needs. And someone who lives an hour away from the nearest church is not obligated to attend extra-liturgical ceremonies like exposition of the Eucharist. But if we really love Jesus—who, even more than our own spouse, is *our true soulmate*—we need to make sacrifices for Him. "What use is life to me if I do not spend it entirely in loving and pleasing [God]," St Alphonsus asks.

Often times, to show appreciation for his wife, a husband will buy her flowers. A wife, in turn, will cook him dinner. Every relationship is a two-way street. You get out of it what you put into it. The same is true with God. In visiting the Blessed Sacrament, we show Him how much we care for Him. "For those who are in love there is no greater pleasure than to be in one another's company," St Alphonsus observes. He reiterates this point by observing that if a king were to live in a village of a poor shepherd, and the shepherd did not visit him, despite knowing the king came just so he could speak to him, the shepherd would betray an immense amount of ingratitude. Yet this is exactly what happens when we fail to spend time with Christ at adoration. "It is only those who do not love Him who grow weary in His presence," St Alphonsus explains.

When I was growing up, my dad would often tell me, "the squeaky wheel gets the grease." His point was that in order to get what you want, you need to speak up. You can't just be a bump on a log and expect things to change. The same is true in the spiritual life. If we continually visit Our Lord and petition

Him with our desires, we'll soon have our prayers answered. If we don't spend time with Christ, we shouldn't expect much in return. "The sheep that remain near their shepherd are more favored and receive more fondling than the others," St Alphonsus observes. Below is a prayer he composed for Catholics to say in front of the Blessed Sacrament:

> My Lord Jesus Christ, because Thou lovest us so much, Thou remainest night and day in this sacrament, full of pity and love, awaiting, calling, and welcoming all who come to visit Thee.
>
> I believe that Thou art present in the sacrament of the altar. I adore Thee from the depths of my heart. I thank Thee for the many graces Thou hast given me, and especially for having given me Mary, Thy Mother, as my advocate, and for having called me to visit Thee here.
>
> I speak to Thy most amiable and loving heart for three reasons: to thank Thee for this great gift; to atone for all the insults which Thou have received; and to compensate by my adoration the lack of it in all those places where the Blessed Sacrament is the least reverenced and most abandoned.
>
> My Jesus, I love thee with my whole heart. I am sorry that I have so often offended Thy infinite goodness. With the help of Thy grace, I resolve to offend Thee no more. I give Thee my will, my affections, my desires, and all that is mine; do with me and with all that belongs to me whatever Thou wish. I ask for nothing but Thy holy love, final perseverance, and the perfect fulfillment of Thy Will.
>
> I recommend to Thee the souls in purgatory, especially those who were most devoted to this sacrament and to Mary. I also recommend to Thee all poor sinners. And lastly,

my beloved Savior, I unite all my affections with those of Thy most loving heart, and thus united, I offer them to Thy eternal Father, and in Thy name I beg Him to accept and grant them. Amen.

Considerations

- Where is the nearest adoration chapel? When is it open? What day and time can I visit Our Lord there this week? If there isn't one, how can I help start one?

- Jesus is truly present in the Eucharist. How can I follow St Alphonsus' advice on preparing to receive Him at Mass? How can I follow St Alphonsus' advice on thanking Him afterwards?

- Do I go to Mass every weekend? If not, why not? If I do, am I attentive to what is happening? Does my behavior indicate I truly believe Jesus is there? Where is the closest Latin Mass and when can I attend it in the next month?

- St Alphonsus teaches that confession frees us from sin and makes us children of God. When was the last time I went to confession? More than three months ago? I vow here and now that I will go to confession in the next two weeks.

- What are two things I can do to help family, friends, and others better understand and, ultimately, embrace the Church's teachings on the Eucharist? Do I need to re-study the Catechism?

CHAPTER 5

RELIGIOUS LIFE

There's an unfortunate tendency among Catholics today to view their parish priest as a sort of quality-control inspector, as a sort of regular Joe who merely presides over Mass by making sure all the moving parts are running as planned.

According to St Alphonsus, priests are greater not only than the most powerful kings and rulers of the earth, but even the angels. "God cannot raise a man to a greater elevation than by conferring on him the sacerdotal dignity [of the priesthood]," he says. He gives two reasons for this. The first is that priests—and priests alone—call down from Heaven the Bread of Life at Mass. Not Eucharistic ministers. Not altar servers. Not lectors. The priest. "The dignity of the priest is ... estimated from the power that he has over the real and the mystic body of Jesus Christ." When priests "pronounce the words of consecration the Incarnate Word has obliged Himself to obey and to come into their hands under the Sacramental Species." This means that "a priest gives greater honor to God than all the Angels and Saints, along with the Blessed Virgin Mary, have given or shall give to Him." For "their worship cannot be of infinite value, like that which the priest celebrating on the altar offers to God." Second, priests have the power to forgive sins, an act that frees a soul from eternal punishment and allows it to be in friendship with God.

St Alphonsus provides the following commentary on the priesthood that is worth meditating on:

> 'Nothing,' says St Ambrose, 'is more excellent in this world.' [The priesthood] transcends, says St Bernard, 'all the dignities of kings, of emperors, and of Angels.' According to St Ambrose, the dignity of the priest far exceeds that of kings, as the value of gold surpasses that of lead. The reason is, because the power of kings extends only to temporal goods and to the bodies of men, but the power of the priest extends to spiritual goods and to the human soul. Hence, says St Clement, 'as much as the soul is more noble than the body, so much is the priesthood more excellent than royalty.' 'Princes,' says St John Chrysostom, 'have the power of binding, but they bind only the bodies, while the priest binds the souls.'

When I read these words for the first time, my understanding of the Church changed immediately. Scales fell from my eyes. They made me realize the unique role priests play in God's Divine Plan. They allowed me, in other words, to see that the priesthood is far above the laity in dignity and in purpose, and that priests have been chosen by God to play an essential role in salvation history, and that it's not a form of "clericalism" to view priests in this manner either.

What further opened my eyes to the beauty of the priesthood was what St Alphonsus says about it in comparison to Mary:

> The power of the priest surpasses that of the Blessed Virgin Mary; for, although this divine Mother can pray for us, and by her prayers obtain whatever she wishes, yet she cannot absolve a Christian from even the smallest sin. 'The Blessed Virgin was eminently more perfect than the Apostles,' says Innocent III. 'It was, however, not to her, but

only to the Apostles, that the Lord entrusted the keys of the kingdom of Heaven.'

These remarks shouldn't be interpreted to mean that the Catholic Church is a mindless cult that worships its priests. Catholics today know all too well that God uses imperfect vessels as His instruments. Some clergy have scandalously given in to their own dominant faults and have brought shame to Christ's Church by abusing their office in various ways. Others twist the Church's doctrines to fit their progressive ideology. This has had disastrous consequences for the Church (and world) as a whole. St Alphonsus explains how by stating the following:

> The good morals and the salvation of the people depend on good pastors. If there is a good priest in charge of the parish, you will soon see devotion flourishing and people frequenting the Sacraments and honoring the practice of mental prayer. Hence the proverb: like pastor, like parish.[26]

It shouldn't come as a surprise, then, that a 2015 Pew Research poll found that one in four Catholics living in the United States has had a divorce, that four in ten have cohabitated with a member of the opposite sex, and that sixty-six percent don't believe it's a sin to use birth control.[27] Bad priests are, at root, the reason why this has occurred.

Regardless of the terrible examples set by liberal clergy (many of whom should either be laicized or officially censured by the Vatican), Catholics need to retain a proper understanding of the *office* of the priesthood. As St Francis of Assisi once said, "If I saw

---

26 Jean-Baptiste Chautard, *The Soul of the Apostolate* (Rockford, IL: TAN Books, 2008), 41.

27 Alan Cooperman, ed. "U.S. Catholics Open to Non-Traditional Families," Pew Research Center, 2 Sep 2015, https://www.pewforum.org/2015/09/02/u-s-catholics-open-to-non-traditional-families/.

an Angel and a priest, I would bend my knee first to the priest and then to the Angel."

Considering a Vocation

After the Second Vatican Council, the Catholic Church experienced a massive, worldwide drop-off, not only in priests, but also in women religious. To characterize what's happened as a tragedy is to put it lightly. It's essential in the years ahead for young men to consider giving themselves to God first, instead of to a woman. The Church cannot survive without priests.

I myself visited a Latin Mass seminary in the United States a mere fifteen months after first encountering St Alphonsus' writings. I simply wanted to know if God wished to use my new-found zeal for a greater purpose. When I pulled up to the entrance for my week-long stay, I parked my car and said a quick prayer. "Lord, I am dust and to dust I shall return. Do with me what Thou will."

The week began with a sense of calmness but also uncertainty. I was willing to let God show me He wanted me to be a priest, but I wasn't sure how that would happen in a matter of days. I decided to keep a journal about my visit. Each night before bed, I wrote about how the day went and what I thought God was telling me. Here is a snippet from what I wrote on my first night:

> Met my host today. His name is Michael. He is a sixth-year seminarian. Super welcoming. He is helping me find my way around the building and get used to the daily schedule of classes and prayers. I love praying Compline. It is so melodious, almost hypnotic. It is strange seeing so many cassocks in one place. There is a real sense of hierarchy here. Everyone is here on their own accord. God is moving all of them to do His will in different ways. This is a holy place.

As the week progressed, I found myself constantly going to the chapel down the hall from my room. It was a small but beautiful space. The wooden altar was dark brown and adorned with gold paint. I would sit there, alone, for an hour every morning and afternoon. I was receiving the most intense consolations of my life. It was like I was created by God to just meditate on Him in that chapel.

On the third day, I began to feel more at home. The newness of my visit had worn off and I had gotten used to the ebbs and flows of seminary life. In the afternoons, I would go for long walks on nearby dirt roads with some of the second and third-year seminarians. We discussed current events but mostly talked about how and why they decided to pursue a vocation.

Some of them were raised Traditional Catholics and were home-schooled in their youth. Others hadn't heard of the Latin Mass until their twenties. Most of them said they "just wanted to try out" the seminary. "It wasn't super mysterious or difficult to make a decision to enter," one young man informed me. "It was a matter of being open to whatever God wants from me. I want to please Him."

By mid-week I began to seriously consider whether God was calling me to the priesthood. Here's what I wrote in my journal on day four: "Why can't I be a priest? What's holding me back? Surely, I can do this. Why shouldn't I do this? After all, it's not like I have a girlfriend back home or a career I need to run back to. I can definitely see myself here."

To my surprise, when I woke up the next morning, I started feeling anxious. I confided to a fifth-year seminarian that I was increasingly at peace with the idea of becoming a priest but that I was nervous, even scared, about consecrating the Eucharist at Mass.

"We're all unworthy," he calmly explained, "but God may be asking you to do this. If that is what He wants, there's nothing more you can do. You shouldn't be afraid. You just need to respond to that call."

After that conversation, I went back to my room to be alone. I'd been sitting in on so many classes and talking to as many seminarians as I could that I simply needed a break. I laid on my bed and was looking out my window when I heard God speak to me: "Feed my sheep."

"Feed my sheep?" I thought.

"Feed my sheep."

Now, it wasn't like God whispered those exact words in my ear in a deep, baritone voice (as is often portrayed in movies). But when I was looking out my window on that warm spring day, those were the only words I could think about. They were literally impressing themselves onto my soul. I immediately began to weep.

"You really want me, Lord?" I said out loud. "Is this really the life you want for me? Until the day I die? Feed my sheep?"

I left the seminary thinking I'd be back in no time, despite the rector telling me to wait before applying in order to see if what I was experiencing was a momentary flash in the pan or something more. I spent the next year going to adoration, praying in the cemetery, fasting, doing different devotions, and generally preparing myself for a return visit.

When I went back to the seminary for ordinations each of the next two years, I caught up with some of the young men I had met during my visit. Some had been elevated to the priesthood and I wanted to congratulate them and get their first blessing. Others, who weren't yet ordained, told me they looked forward to the day I would enter.

What Do You Want From Me, Lord?

In the years following my visit, I was more or less convinced God wanted me to become a priest. The thing was, I couldn't get healthy. Or get out of debt. Medical bills were piling up and I wasn't making headway on my student loans. What's more, my spiritual life dried up and I fell back into some old habits. Not keeping up a regular prayer life was the number one cause of that. Matthew 12:43–45 certainly applied to me:

> When an impure spirit comes out of a person, it goes through dry places seeking rest, and finding none, it says, 'I will return to the house I left.' When it arrives, it finds the house unoccupied, swept clean and put in order. It then brings with it seven other spirits more wicked than itself, and they go in and live there, and the last state of that man is made worse than the first.

Despite that, when I went on a work trip to Europe several years later, I visited a group of priests. I approached my stay with the mentality that perhaps *this* is where God wanted me to begin my studies for religious life.

The week began pretty much the same as my five-day Ignatian retreat the year before. I barely slept thanks to my neurological symptoms acting up. Motivation to get out of bed in the morning was also hard to come by, so much so that I missed Mass on several occasions. Furthermore, when we had a Holy Hour, I couldn't concentrate. I was also extremely desolate, especially when praying the Rosary. I even hopped on a computer to check my e-mail and catch up on politics. Eventually, I called the airline to see if I could move up my flight back to the United States three days earlier.

Overall, the week was a disastrous spiritual experience. Amid tears, I begged God, "What do you want from me? What did I do wrong? Did you want me to come here in the first place? Did I make a mistake? What do you want from me now?!" I started thinking that "feed my sheep" meant something entirely different.

When I got back to America I called it quits on pursuing a vocation. My career was rewarding and I was traveling to different parts of the country on an almost monthly basis. I was also interviewing influential public figures and making good money. What more could a thirty-something bachelor want?

Despite that, there have been times when I've reconsidered the priesthood in recent years. I needn't present all of those scenarios in this space, beyond what I've already written. As of the publication of this book, I am an unmarried, single man. In your charity, can you pray to the Sacred Heart of Jesus, Our Lady of Perpetual Help, St Joseph, St Alphonsus, St Thérèse, and St Padre Pio so that I will soon enter the state in life God has always desired for me?

Priestly Men

When discerning a vocation, it is of the utmost importance to know that the priesthood isn't about making people *feel* good. Nor is it about preaching in fancy cathedrals. It's about pleasing God and doing His Will regardless of your feelings. Priests today must walk by faith and not by sight and know that living out their vocation will likely result in them being canceled, mocked, and forced to carry out their ministry in a way entirely at odds with how their predecessors did.

Priests just don't grow on trees either. Nor do they pop up out of the ground. They come from families. Parents have the obligation of raising future priests by providing them with a Catholic home life. One way they can do that is to have large families, and not just one boy and one girl. "In general, for every three children, there is one vocation," St Alphonsus once remarked.

St Alphonsus teaches that parents should always encourage their sons and daughters to consider the seminary or convent if they have the inclination for it. Those who hinder or dissuade a child from a vocation are guilty of a "double sin," he says. Not only are they sinning against charity, they're sinning against piety by not assisting their vocation.

This is an interesting observation by St Alphonsus, as his own father was initially opposed to him being a priest. In his many writings, St Alphonsus observes that for a priest to follow Christ he must put his family second, no matter the cost. "A priest must divest himself of attachment to relatives," he writes. "We must, says a learned author, disown [our families] in whatever is opposed to our spiritual advancement."

The priesthood is also not to be entered lightly. According to St Alphonsus, God has declared His wrath against those who wish to rule in His Church without being called by Him. "He who takes holy orders without a call from God is convicted of theft." Quoting St Gregory, he notes that, "the hand that must wash away the stains and defilements of others must not be polluted." How can priests live in such a way as to honor their office and to not "pollute" their hands? St Alphonsus has plenty to say on this subject, though I'll reference only a small sample of his remarks.

"By a single look of curiosity at Bathsheba, David miserably fell into the sins of adultery, homicide, and scandal," St Alphonsus wrote in a letter to priests. "A deliberate glance at a person of a different sex often enkindles an infernal spark, which consumes the soul." He further explains that:

> The priest should ... exhibit gravity in his dress [and] gravity in his countenance: in order to set an example of modesty,

he must keep his eyes cast down, not only when he is on the altar and in the church, but also in all places in which there are women ... he must carefully abstain from uttering certain worldly maxims, and certain jests that are contrary to modesty.

He continues: "it is also necessary for the priest to abstain from every species of detraction [and] to avoid familiar intercourse with seculars. The conversations of seculars breathe an infectious air, which, as St Basil says, 'gradually destroys the health of the soul.'"

"A priest," he also warns, "should disregard his conveniences, his interests, and amusements; he should consider that from the day that he has received the priesthood, he belongs not to himself, but to God; and should attend only to the interests of God." A priest must undertake "all his actions for the sole purpose of pleasing God."

I can only imagine the horror in St Alphonsus' eyes if he were alive today and saw the behavior of so many priests outside of church as well as inside it when they offer irreverent Masses. He would also be appalled by the fact that so many priests no longer wear their cassocks and instead walk around in t-shirts, polos, and shorts.

Raising Future Saints

As previously mentioned, St Alphonsus' father, Don Joseph Liguori, opposed, and even attempted to prevent, his son from becoming a priest. With time, he came to understand that it was God's Will that he receive holy orders. "O my son, how grateful I am to you!" he told him years later. "You have taught me really to know God. I bless you and thank you a thousand times for embracing a state so holy and pleasing to God."[28]

Given the immense drop-off in vocations over the past sixty years, one can't help but wonder if more parents are disincentivizing their children from considering religious life. Sadly, it's not difficult to imagine this is what's happening, as it seems parents today are more interested in familiarizing their children with Disney characters, sports teams, and video games than in reading them the lives of the saints, praying the rosary together, and having dinner with the parish priest. As a result, by the time children reach the age of reason, they know more about athletes and fictional "superheroes" than the names of the twelve apostles or the great popes of the past. Simply put, God is not being given a chance to even call young people into His service anymore.

St Alphonsus often wrote about family life and the duties parents have toward their children. "A father owes two obligations to his children: He is bound to provide for their corporal wants, and to educate them in the habits of virtue." Scripture, he adds, teaches that "when a father observes the divine law, both he and his children shall prosper." But when a father doesn't, and the son is addicted to blasphemies and certain vices, "we have reason to suspect that such too was the character of the father." Origen, he frighteningly recalls, "says that on the day of the judgment parents will have to render an account for all the sins of their children."

St Thérèse of Lisieux's parents, Louis and Zélie Martin, had ten children, five of whom died in early life. Of those that survived, all became nuns, St Thérèse being the youngest. Louis and Zélie are often held up as an example *par excellence* of what Catholic parents can and should be. Not only did they live holy, prayer-filled lives—instilling in their daughters a love for

---

28 D.F. Miller and L.X. Aubin, *Saint Alphonsus Liguori: Doctor of the Church* (Charlotte, NC: TAN Books, 2012), 37–38.

sanctity and humility—but they also knew how to *let go* of their children, emotionally speaking, so they could serve God in the cloister. Louis and Zélie (as well as Alphonsus' own mother) no doubt heeded the following words of St Alphonsus:

> Religious parents teach [their children] the acts which ought to be made every morning after rising. They teach them, first, to thank God for having preserved their life during the night; second, to offer to God all the good actions they will perform and all the pains they shall suffer during the day; third, to implore of Jesus Christ and Most Holy Mary to preserve them from all sin during the day.

St Alphonsus provides plenty of other practical tips for parents seeking to do the Will of God as well. "A good father should often assemble his children, and instill into them the holy fear of God." They will "inquire after the conduct of his children." What ruin "is brought upon his children by the father who teaches them worldly maxims!"

St Alphonsus further instructs fathers in particular to forbid their children to visit places where their virtue might be exposed to danger. A father "should not permit his daughters to be alone with men, whether young or old." He must also "remove from his house romance novels that pervert young persons, and all bad books which contain pernicious maxims, tales of obscenity, or of profane love." In modern parlance, this would mean removing from the home immodest films and other influences that tempt young adults to impurity.

Parents should "prohibit to their children all games which bring destruction on their families and on their own souls, and also masks, scandalous comedies, and certain dangerous conversations and parties of pleasure," St Alphonsus further advises. "Bad companions are the ruin of young persons." One here thinks of modern teenage "dating," especially high school prom and other events that more or less entice adolescents to act as if they were married adults.

Ultimately, St Alphonsus instructs parents to train their children to adopt good religious habits so they'll retain them when they grow up. "Make every evening an examination of conscience and an act of contrition," he recommends. If a father frequents the sacraments, prays the Rosary, abstains from obscene language, avoids detraction, and lives a holy life, "you shall see that your sons will" as well, for children, St Alphonsus observes, "are like apes; they do what they see their parents do."

As previously noted, vocations don't pop up out of the ground. They come from families. Who knows, maybe God wants your son to be the next St Alphonsus, and your daughter to be the next St Thérèse? God needs priests and nuns in order to grow His Church. Will you and your spouse make it difficult for your children to hear God's call? Or will you create a home life that makes it easy for them to say "yes" to religious life?

"Had Don Joseph succeeded in his many schemes to turn Alphonsus aside from his vocation, the world would be lacking many a saint, and hundreds of thousands of souls would not have had the extraordinary graces that were to come through his Congregation," one 20th century biography of St Alphonsus points out. These words should serve as a stark reminder of the immense responsibilities parents have in raising their children.

Preaching Like St Alphonsus

Before moving on, an important note should be made of what St Alphonsus says about preaching, as it's not uncommon today to see many Catholic priests act like Protestant preachers in the delivery of their sermons.

During his own ministry, St Alphonsus more or less revolutionized preaching. Rather than adopting the long, highly verbose style that had been prevalent at the time, Alphonsus stressed the need for simplicity and brevity. "I have never preached a sermon which the poorest old woman in the congregation could not understand," he once said.[29] He adopted this method as a result of his many interactions in the neglected communities he visited. His experiences, in other words, made him realize that a more straightforward preaching manner was necessary.

Priests should preach, St Alphonsus says, first and foremost with modesty:

> One should avoid gestures that are affected or too uniform, that are always the same, or so impetuous as to give to the body an excessive agitation by moving inordinately the hands, the head, or the eyes.... It is ordinarily the right hand that makes the gestures.... One should not raise the hand higher than the head, nor extend it too much.... The movement of the head should be regulated by the movement of the hand by turning the head in the same direction.

Priests should also draw attention not to themselves but rather to their words, which should be said in a way as if they were coming from the lips of Jesus Christ. All of a priest's "words, thoughts, desires, and actions must be an exercise of Divine Love."

Priests should likewise keep their sermons simple and not try to impress their audience with eloquent or learned phrases. "When the word of God is adulterated by studied elegance of expression it becomes feeble and enervated," St Alphonsus teaches.

Sermons should not be longer than thirty minutes and should focus on no more than two or three main points. "Some priests have the admirable ability to bring in the Blessed Virgin Mary into every sermon," he once remarked. He himself did this by preaching about Mary on Saturdays. He also required

29 Enzo Lodi, *Saints of the Roman Calendar* (New York: Alba House, 1992), 208.

Redemptorist priests to give sermons on her mercy during their missions.[30] "Bad preachers and bad confessors are the ruin of the world," he remarked.

Priests must be careful, he adds, to not preach about God's justice so frequently as to leave the faithful discouraged. They must inspire them to not give up on the journey to perfection. "The great object [of preaching]," St Alphonsus summarizes, "should be to explain nakedly and simply the eternal truths, the importance of salvation, and to lay before the people the illusions of the devil, the dangers of perdition, and the means to be adopted in some particular cases that may occur."

A Pastor of Souls

Being a priest is not easy. Sacrificing one's life for others is extremely demanding, both spiritually and physically. Aside from preaching sound doctrine from the pulpit, reverently offering Mass, and being an example to others every second of the day, priests have to know how to act toward each and every person who enters the confessional so as to lead them out of sin and into holiness. Catholics have to pray for their priests!

St Alphonsus correctly notes that being a confessor is both the most important and most difficult role of a priest, as it demands knowledge "of almost all the sciences." As the patron saint of confessors, St Alphonsus is the perfect priest for clergy to seek advice from on this subject. His *Guide for Confessors* is a must-own.

St Alphonsus plainly states that a confessor, "should be full of charity. This charity should be shown, in the first place, in the way everyone is welcome." Good confessors "know precisely that this Sacrament was instituted more for sinners than for pious

30 Rengers & Bunson, 656.

people." He laments, however, that "some priests wish only to hear the confessions of the devout or of the people with social standing." If "some poor sinner comes, they reluctantly hear their confession and then send the person away in an abrupt manner." This odious practice has the terrible effect of making laity develop a hatred for confession and of being scared to go again.

In order to be like Christ, confessors should show special solicitude to souls ensnared by particularly evil sins. "Welcome him with kindness and even with a note of triumph at the gain he has been fortunate enough to snatch from the devil's grasp," he advises. Priests should also share words of encouragement to those who are nervous or uncertain of themselves, while also giving penances that are not overly burdensome but rather fitting to their state in life.

What else should confessors do? They should not worry about those who are waiting in line for confession. They need only to focus on the soul currently in front of them. In order to root out sin, priests should also induce penitents to pray and to "turn their thoughts to God" in both the morning and evening, using a book of meditations if necessary. "In order to win [sinners] back to God," St Alphonsus writes, "[good confessors] must receive them with deep love and let them see how much he wants to help them."

A Priest's Life

As head of the Redemptorists, St Alphonsus composed letters to both male clergy and women religious (his book *The True Spouse of Jesus Christ* was addressed specifically to nuns). He referred to his priests as his "brothers" and told them they were far dearer to him than his own relatives. He often reminded them to thank God for calling them out of the world. "These graces are not given to everybody."

In one particular letter, he grieved over the Church being in a state of "relaxation and confusion." He also wished that the pope would name truly pious men to important dioceses. One can't help but wonder what words he would use to describe the Church (and the scandalous individuals elevated to prominent positions in Her) today!

In his many letters, St Alphonsus pleaded with higher-ranking clergy to act with great pastoral care. "It would be a blessing if all superiors could imitate [Jesus Christ], for superiors should always be as kind as possible to those who are under them. If something needs to be done, they should request rather than command." A superior "should be kind even when pointing out faults," he continues. "Firmness may occasionally be necessary ... still, we should be careful about correcting someone harshly or in anger, for that does more harm than good."

St Alphonsus also urged those who were overseeing seminarians to not be excessive in their demands. "I want the students to be strong in health, and I do not mind their losing two hours of study," he once wrote. "In the evening ... let them go outdoors and have at least one hour's remission." One biographer explains that when read in their totality, St Alphonsus' personal letters indicate he was "kind, considerate, fatherly, even indulgent, and above all, very human in his dealings with others."

Given that many priests today have grown lukewarm in living out their vocation (or, at the very least, are confused about what it means to be a priest), it's worth spending a few additional moments on what St Alphonsus teaches about how priests ought to behave.

In his book *Dignity and Duties of the Priest*, St Alphonsus covers everything from table manners and the interior life to proper recreation and relations with laity. "Games of amusement ... are but little suited to a minister of God." Priests should have a special solicitude for the sick and imprisoned, and to overcome attachments to pride. "It is necessary to guard against glorying in any good that we may do," he says. A "proud spiritual man is the worst of robbers; because he usurps not earthly goods, but the glory of God."

St Alphonsus further advises clergy to associate with and read about the lives of holy priests so they will be edified by their example. What's more, a priest should be modest "but without affectation, severity, or fastidiousness; and he should always wear the cassock." Priests, he adds, must "flee from worldly conversation" and "be quiet and gentle at home" while being "edifying in church, especially during the public offices." The Council of Tours, he also recalls, "tells priests that they should guard against everything that can offend the eyes or the ears." The priest ought to give "an example of modesty in all things: modesty in looks, modesty in his gait, modesty in his conversation, particularly by saying little, and by speaking as a priest ought to speak."

Again, how sad St Alphonsus would be to see priests today doing the exact opposite of what he and the other great churchmen of the past instructed. How disappointed he would be to learn that men of the cloth in the 21st century are indulging in television, wasting time on smart phones, using debased language, gossiping, frequenting movie theaters and the finest restaurants, and allowing their eyes, ears, and taste buds to be satisfied beyond all measure. "All the saints have thirsted after penitential austerities, and have sought to macerate the flesh to the utmost of their power," he once wrote. "St Francis Borgia, even when a secular ... was content with bread and herbs."

At the same time, St Alphonsus was keenly aware that priests are human beings scarred by Original Sin, and that moderation is undoubtedly needed. "I do not say that during recreation you should always speak on serious topics," he concedes. "Laugh, amuse yourself, speak even on entertaining subjects, but preserve recollection, by interiorly making occasional acts of the love of

God, or petitions for His graces." It is also licit, he admits, to enjoy good tasting food. Still, it seems obvious that he would harshly rebuke the many clerics today who opt for the bare minimum in the spiritual life. A soul that's inflamed with Divine Love "no longer has any sense of the things of the world," he writes. It wants to "think only of God, to speak only of God." Priests who do not take these words seriously cause grave scandal and put their eternal salvation at risk.

When he was ordained at the age of thirty, St Alphonsus vowed to live a life of complete self-denial. "Always ask for the love of God, and for the grace to belong entirely to him," he told his priests. Below is an abbreviated list of just some of the resolutions he made. They act as a small catechism for clergy interested in following his holy example:

- I am a priest; my dignity is above that of the angels. I should then lead a life of angelic purity, and I am obliged to strive for this by all possible means.

- I offer to the Eternal Father Jesus Christ, His Son: it is then my duty to clothe myself with the virtues of Jesus Christ, that I may become fit for my office.

- Christian people see in me a minister of reconciliation, a mediator between God and man; consequently I must always keep myself in the grace and friendship of God.

- The faithful desire to see in me a model of the virtues to which they should aspire; I must then be edifying always and under all circumstances.

- Poor sinners that have lost the light of grace come to me to be spiritually resuscitated: I must therefore aid them by my prayers, exhortations, and good example.

- To defend religion and fight against error and impiety, one must have knowledge. I will then strive, by every means within my reach, to acquire the necessary knowledge.

- Human respect and worldly friendships dishonor the priesthood; I will then avoid them.

- Ambition and self-interest have often caused priests to lose their faith; I must then abhor these vices as sources of reprobation.

- Gravity should accompany charity in a priest; I will then be prudent and reserved, especially with regard to women, without being proud, rough, or disdainful.

- I should seek only the Glory of God, my own sanctification, and the salvation of souls; consequently, I must achieve these ends though it should cost my life.

- I am a priest; it is my duty to inspire virtue in all with whom I come in contact, and to glorify Jesus Christ, the eternal High-priest.

St Alphonsus says you can tell a priest has truly handed himself over to God if he possess the following characteristics:

First, they do not get upset if they do not obtain the results they set out to achieve, because they are at peace in the realization that, if it is not what God wants, they should not want it either. Second, they are as pleased with the good achieved by others as they are with their own successes. Third, they express no preferences about the kind of work they do, but are content with whatever is decided by obedience. Fourth, when the work is done, they seek neither approval nor thanks from others.

Preparing for Holy Orders

"If you are called by God to leave the world ... seek to execute it as promptly as you can," St Alphonsus recommends.

> I abandoned the world, in which unfortunately, I lived until I was six-and-twenty years of age. Fortunate indeed you will be if you can detach yourself from it at an earlier period and give yourself without reserve to that Lord who has given Himself without reserve to you.

The devil uses many tools to prevent pious souls from pursuing religious life. Sometimes, he turns their own parents against them. Other times, friends, old acquaintances, past enjoyments, and dominant faults stymie their resolve. The end result being that some vocations are, in fact, lost and souls end up living at odds with the life God wanted for them. St Alphonsus argues that this puts them at a heightened risk of damnation. "As God has called you, you will never have peace, if you remain in the world."

In an effort to encourage young men to consider the priesthood, St Alphonsus would ask them to imagine themselves on their deathbed and to reflect on the joy they will have knowing they spent their whole life in complete service to God. Then, he asks them to imagine the remorse they will feel for having refused God's graces. "I curse those days in which ... I followed my own will," he said of his own past. "All is folly: feasts, theaters, parties of pleasure, amusements—these are the goods of this world, but goods which are filled with the bitterness of gall and with sharp thorns."

St Alphonsus provides a number of recommendations to those who are pursuing a vocation. "Keep perfectly recollected, detaching [yourselves] from everything of this world." Perform at least thirty minutes of mental prayer every morning and frequently receive Holy Communion, always being sure to ask Jesus and

Mary for perseverance. "One day of amusement, a word from a friend, a thought of fear...suffices to bring to nought all our resolutions of retiring from the world," he writes. "We ought during this time to think of nothing but prayer and frequenting the sacraments, and to be nowhere but at home and in church."

Young men and women should not be under the illusion that life at the seminary or convent will be an earthly paradise, he also warns. In fact, it will likely be rather challenging. "To suffer contempt either from Superiors or from companions is a thing unavoidable even in the most holy communities," St Alphonsus notes. "Let [aspirants to religious life] not imagine that [they] will be exempt from other temptations and trials."

God allows those who are seeking holy orders to encounter these challenges to help them grow in patience. Those who "cannot quietly put up with contempt and contradiction" will "gain little in religion," St Alphonsus adds. God permits "even among saints [that] there should exist, though without their fault, certain natural antipathies, or at least, a certain diversity of character among subjects of the greatest piety, which will cause them to suffer many contradictions."

What further advice does St Alphonsus have for seminarians (and novices) pursuing religious life? "He who does not resolve to suffer and to overcome himself in the things contrary to his inclinations, will never be able to enjoy this true peace," he teaches. "Provided there is no evident sin, he ought in every command imposed on him to obey blindly and without examination." A student "must always keep his mind ready to do all that for which he feels the greatest [repugnance]."

St Alphonsus also makes the important point that "no one can claim he has been called by God if he receives holy orders while still not yet free from habitual vice, especially against chastity." Those who aspire to the clerical state should therefore communicate to their superior any temptations they have:

Let him who wishes to enter religion not forget to resolve to become a saint, and to suffer every exterior and interior pain, in order to be faithful to God, and not to lose his vocation. And if he be not resolved to this, I exhort him not to deceive the Superior and himself, and not to enter at all, for this is a sign that he is not called.

Finally, St Alphonsus says that pride and ambition "disfigures" a religious community. "One must first place under foot all self-esteem, by desiring and embracing every imaginable contempt that he may meet with in religion." He should be willing "to see others ... preferred to himself." St Alphonsus continues: "In the monastery he will not have the entertainments of music, theaters, and balls, but he will have God to console him and to make him enjoy peace." The soul "is created only for God ... all the pleasures and riches of the earth cannot give true peace." Quoting St Scholastica, St Alphonsus predicts that "if men knew the peace that good religious enjoy, the whole world would become a monastery."

The Nun's Story

God could have chosen any number of ways to establish the Redemptorist Order. He decided to use a woman.

Giulia Crostarosa was born in Naples on October 31, 1696, just one month after St Alphonsus. The tenth of twelve children, she entered the Carmelites with her sister Ursula in 1718. History would remember her as Sr Maria Celeste.

In 1722, Fr Thomas Falcoia, a Naples priest who belonged to the Congregation of Pious Workers, preached a retreat for her community. She was so impressed with him that she asked him to be her spiritual adviser. When her convent closed, she and Ursula (as well as their younger sister Giovanna) were invited by Fr Falcoia to join a group of nuns he oversaw in the town of Scala. They arrived in 1724. While yet a novice, she experienced visions of Our Lord. On April 25, 1725, Jesus told her that He wished to found a new congregation, one that would serve as a living memory to His work of salvation and love for mankind.

Many, including Falcoia, were doubtful of Maria Celeste's claims. After years of bureaucratic roadblocks, he delegated the matter to a young Fr Alphonsus, to whom he had grown closer. In September 1730, Alphonsus arrived in Scala. Using the skills he acquired as a lawyer, he conducted a full investigation. He resolved the matter so efficiently over the ensuing month that it was decided the new rule would be introduced to the community the following year. On the Feast of Pentecost in 1731, the Order of the Most Holy Redeemer (what is now called the Redemptoristine Nuns) was established.

Despite the great good that came from Maria Celeste's visions, God was not done using her as His instrument. On October 3, 1731, she had still more revelations. In one of them, she saw St Francis of Assisi and Fr Alphonsus conversing with Christ Himself. She understood that God wanted Alphonsus to lead a parallel group of priests. She wrote down what she witnessed and gave it to Falcoia, who had been consecrated a bishop the previous year.

Although somewhat hesitant about the matter, Falcoia joyfully embraced the possibility of such a venture. Alphonsus, too, was anxious, but after consulting many learned and pious priests—and after speaking with Maria Celeste—he resolved to undertake the matter. The decision devastated his father, who believed that evangelizing peasants in the remote Italian countryside was a waste of his talents. "It was the strongest temptation I ever had," Alphonsus later said of needing to leave behind his family and native village.

In November 1732, Alphonsus set out from Naples to Scala, where, in the guest house on the nun's property, he founded the Congregation of the Most Holy Redeemer. His new community conducted its first liturgical ceremonies on Sunday, November 9, with Falcoia presiding.

"More than once a day they scourged themselves," one biographer informs us of those initial companions, who counted less than a half dozen. They engaged in other mortifications as well, including the wearing of hair shirts and sharp chains around their arms, legs, and bodies. Alphonsus chastised himself throughout his life.

But the excitement soon faded. Less than six months later, all but one lay-brother had left the order after failing to reach consensus on practical matters. Praying the Divine Office in common and organizing schools were particular points of contention. Maria Celeste herself resigned in May 1733 after complications arose with Falcoia. Five years later, however, she founded a Redemptoristine convent in Foggia, where she died with a reputation for holiness on September 14, 1755. Her body is still venerated there today.

Women Religious

As can be seen, St Alphonsus had a special charism for assisting women religious. He would often visit, conduct retreats, write letters, and, of course, pray for them. "I rejoice to see the new institute making steady progress," Falcoia informed him of Maria Celeste's order in November 1731. "And the merit is all yours, because it is you who carry the burden of it."

St Alphonsus frequently wrote on topics relevant not only to religious and single women but to mothers as well. Never one to mince words, he once said:

How is it possible to excuse mothers who allow their daughters to keep company with persons in love with them? They desire to see their daughters married, but they do not care whether they commit sin. These are the mothers of whom David speaks, who, for the interest of the family, immolate their daughters to the devil.

St Alphonsus was particularly keen on encouraging young women to pursue religious life. "[God] offers you two immense advantages which the world cannot give—peace of soul in this life, and paradise in the next," he wrote to one who was asking about the convent. He would also strongly advise them against marriage:

What time has a married woman for thinking upon God? [She] has to think of rearing her children, of pleasing her husband, and her husbands' relatives; whence, as the Apostle says, her heart is divided between God, her husband, and her children. Her husband must be attended to; the children cry and scream, and are continually asking for a thousand things…

How many [married women] will say … 'I would wish for retirement in order to spend a little time in mental prayer, but the affairs of the family and of the house, which is always in confusion, do not permit this.… My unceasing occupations, the care of children, the frequent visits of friends, keep me confined to the house.…'

"Oh," he also observed, "how many cruel husbands are there … who when first married promised great things, but shortly afterwards ceased to be husbands, and became tyrants of their wives, treating them not as companions but as slaves?" Married persons are in "continual torment" and are so "attached to earthly goods, they reflect but little on spiritual things."

Too often women today are encouraged to show off the bodies God has given them in exchange for money and fame. But by exposing themselves, they turn their back on the twin virtues of modesty and humility, traits St Alphonsus teaches are essential to uniting our wills to God's Will. Feminism, meanwhile, tells women to adopt masculine traits, thereby tricking them into thinking that if they don't do the same tasks men do they will lead incomplete lives. This is completely false, St Alphonsus maintains. "Consider the unhappy lot of so many ladies of fortune, so many princesses and queens, who in the world have been attended, praised, honored, and most adored." The "greatest happiness" belongs to "the lot of those maidens who consecrate themselves to Jesus Christ... they are not bound to earth by love of children, or men, or dress, or gallantry."

In his writings addressed specifically to women religious, St Alphonsus reiterates much of the spiritual advice he gives to priests. "If all nuns were obedient, every convent would be a paradise." Failing to "conquer yourself in small things... will also expose you to the danger of perdition." God "has allowed you to live, not that you may rest, but that you may be persecuted." In one letter, he encouraged total submission of the will:

> If, then, dear Sister, you desire soon to become a saint, consecrate yourself entirely to obedience; divest yourself of all self-will; and endeavor with all your might to obey your Rule and your Superior in the external exercises, and your spiritual Father in whatever regards the interior. It is by obedience and by the absence of self-will that perfect religious are distinguished from the imperfect. The latter do nothing cheerfully, but what pleases self-love and self-will.

"The more you are humbled," he also wrote, "the more closely will you be united with the Heart of our Lord ; for this good

Master loves and enriches with his favors only those that are humble of heart and who embrace humiliations with patience."

Considerations

- Have I thought about giving myself to God by pursuing a vocation? Why not? What is holding me back? Am I too attached to the world? Are these attachments really more important than serving God in His Church? Which state in life will help me save my soul?

- Is marriage truly my calling as a woman? Or does God want me to enter the convent? Do St Alphonsus' writings on women religious appeal to me? Perhaps I should pray to Mary and Sr Maria Celeste to help discern my future?

- Am I raising my children in the Catholic faith so they can more easily pursue a vocation? In what areas am I being too worldly with them? What devotions and religious practices can I introduce to my family so we will all make it to heaven?

- As a seminarian, do I readily accept humiliations and obey orders from my superior? Do I pray for perseverance and detachment from the world, while staying close to Mary? How can I be more like St Alphonsus?

- As a priest, do I conduct myself with the dignity a representative of Christ needs to have at all times? What areas of my ministry need improvement? Which teachings of St Alphonsus can help me become a holier priest?

CHAPTER 6

SIN

It was mentioned in Chapter 4 that the best way to prepare for Communion is to confess our sins to a priest. It should be obvious why sin is evil. At its most basic level, sin is a turning away from God. The Baltimore Catechism defines sin as "any willful thought, word, deed, or omission contrary to the law of God."

But how does sin *really* affect us? And what are some of the tactics the devil uses to ensure we remain in a state of sin?

First, it should be mentioned that according to St Alphonsus—and to all the saints for that matter—God cannot dwell in the soul of a sinner. "When an infant is baptized, the priest says, 'go forth unclean spirit, and give way for the Holy Ghost.' When a man commits a sin, he says 'go forth from me, O Lord, and give place for the devil.'" St Alphonsus further teaches that all things that are irrational obey God: the wind, hail, snow, the sea. But man, a rational creature, says to God when he sins, "I will not obey."

In the Gospel of Matthew, it's related that when Christ arrived in Jerusalem, He instructed His apostles to go into the city and find a donkey tied to a post. St Alphonsus argues that the donkey represents a sinner, a soul chained to the world who is unable to help Our Lord with His mission. Just like how Christ cannot ride a donkey tethered to a rope, God cannot dwell in a soul given over to sin. "A soul that does not love God is not living but dead."

Thirsty Thursdays

I first noticed the real-life impact of sin after I graduated college. The Catholic liberal arts school I attended was a popular destination for students from Catholic high schools across my home state of Michigan. After completing our studies, most of my friends stayed in touch. We attended weddings, met up for golf outings, and made trips to each other's hometowns. But around our mid-twenties, those relationships began to fray. Fewer of us went to homecoming in the fall and weekend get-togethers always ended up being scuttled at the last minute. It's part of life that people move on from old friendships. Some get married. Others re-locate. It's simply the case that you find more meaningful relationships with those in your new city, at work, or at church. As Psalm 127 says, "unless the Lord builds the house, those who labor, labor in vain." That's true for friendships as well.

Like me, many of my classmates lived a sinful life in college—oftentimes, I admit, at my own encouragement. In many ways, college really can be pleasure island. "Young people who remain in the world very easily fall prey to the power of the evil one," St Alphonsus rightly argues. It's amazing that God is so merciful to them, and that He doesn't strike more of them down on the spot for their many sins. If you ask me, it's better for most teenagers to skip college and attend a Christian-themed humanities or trade school. Young girls are better off finding a virtuous husband and mastering the art of household management.

Sadly, many of my classmates didn't make it out of the other side of college with their faith intact. As best I can tell, the residue left on their souls from the Sacraments they received during their Catholic upbringing was largely washed away. They seemed spiritually stunted, in other words. I know this because that was the case for me until my own reversion. Again, I say this not to judge or cast stones. I myself didn't go to Mass during my freshman, sophomore, and junior years. I simply didn't want to be forced to go anymore. In fact, it was a relief not to attend. I convinced myself that I didn't need to worry about all the "rules" the Church put forth. It was only after three years of diligent research, prayer, and deep conversations with friends that, by the grace of God, I started attending Mass every weekend again.

God Abandons the Unrepentant Sinner

It seems to me that our twenties are the decade of our lives most crucial in determining whether or not we'll go to Heaven. It's not that people can't convert later on (many souls, in fact, do), but our twenties are the first test we have to show God that we'll stay true to the faith handed on to us by our parents, or set off on the journey of life following in the footsteps of the world, the flesh, and the devil. If we choose the latter, and continue on in the sinful habits we acquire, it's going to be much more difficult to make a course correction down the road.

The saints are unanimous in teaching that if we turn away from God for an extended period of time, we end up hardening our hearts, blinding ourselves to His Will, and growing weaker in our desire to carry our crosses. By repeatedly rejecting God, we give Him even more of a reason to hide Himself from us, like any spurned lover would (and should) do. St Alphonsus explains how and why this happens by way of a parable:

> The physician visits the sick man, prescribes remedies for him, and makes him sensible of his maladies, but when he sees that his patient does not obey him, he takes leave of him and forsakes him, focusing on those who desire to get healthy. It is thus that God deals with obstinate sinners, after a certain time He speaks little to them and only

assists them with grace sufficient to enable them to save their souls, but they will not save them.

Said another way, God will no longer protect us if we continually put ourselves in situations where we know we will sin or be tempted to sin. "How can we expect that God will be liberal of His favors to us, when we are ungenerous to Him?" St Alphonsus asks.

Ultimately, it's our choice to embrace or reject the great gift God gave us when He blessed us with parents who sent us to Catholic schools and brought us to church growing up. If we return that gift to Him unopened, He'll have no other option than to let us go on our way. On this subject, St Alphonsus says the following:

When the master cuts down the fence of his vineyard, and leaves it open for anyone to enter therein, it is a sign that he considers it not worth cultivating and abandons it. In like manner does God proceed when He forsakes a sinful soul: He takes away from it the hedge of His holy fear, of His light, and of His voice, and hence the soul being blinded and enslaved by its vices, which overpower it, despises everything, the grace of God, Heaven, and admonitions and censures; it thinks lightly even of its own damnation, and thus enveloped in darkness is certain to be lost forever.

What a terrifying thought to be abandoned by Our Lord! It's as if we're being given a foretaste of Hell. But if you think about it, it is right and just that He does this. When we sin by continually putting our will before God's Will, God becomes, according to St Alphonsus, "less liberal in bestowing His graces and helps upon us." How sad that must be for Him who sent His only son to die for us as a total and free gift so we could enjoy eternal bliss with Him.

God's Mercy

Most people are familiar with the story of the prodigal son. A certain man had two sons. One was faithful to him while the other left home and squandered his inheritance. He eventually returned and begged for forgiveness. His elated father threw him a feast, explaining to his other, now jealous son that it was fitting to celebrate his sibling's return, as he'd come back from the jaws of death after living in sin.

The story of the prodigal son illustrates God's mercy. It shows how patient and eager God is to pardon us and how happy He is when we repent from our ways. But make no mistake, just because God has been merciful to others doesn't mean He will be as forgiving to you or me. God judges us on an individual basis. "Although God has patience and waits for the sinner," St Alphonsus observes, "when the day arrives for the measure of his sins to be filled up He will wait for him no longer, but chastise him." He continues:

> The devil may tell you that it matters not whether it be ten or eleven times. But no, that wicked enemy deceives you; the sin which he is tempting you to commit will increase the load of your guilt; it may decide the balance of Divine Justice against you, and you may be condemned for it to the torments of hell.

St Alphonsus also warns:

> To those who abuse [God's] mercy, He punishes with His justice. His mercy does not extend beyond His justice. He who sins and is determined to sin again and is not desirous at all of repentance is not at all worthy of God's mercy. God bears our faults for a time but not forever.

What is the lesson in all this? First, we should return to God as soon as possible. Death comes like a thief in the night. We don't know when or how we'll be called to His judgment. Seriously, how many of your friends, work colleagues, or old classmates from high school are now dead? Did they expect to die so young? Or in the manner in which they passed? Probably not.

Second, as noted earlier, we need to realize that each of us has a set number of sins that God will pardon. Beyond that, we risk provoking His vengeance. "The sinner declares directly to God's face that it is not an evil to disobey His commands," St Alphonsus teaches. God can only take so much mockery.

Confess Your Sins Before It's Too Late

Waiting until your deathbed to confess your sins is a strategy many people seem to adopt. They're under the impression that they'll go out into the world, indulge in a little bit of sin here and there, but that at the end of the day they will still get into Heaven because God will extend His merciful hand to them in their last hours.

This is a lie the devil uses to trick us, St Alphonsus declares. "By loving sin till death, he has loved the danger of his damnation, and therefore God will justly permit him to perish in the danger in which he wished to live till death." Those "unhappy sinners who remain in sin die in a tempest." "St Jerome says, that of a hundred thousand sinners who continue till death in the state of sin, scarcely one shall be saved."

Catholics must take advantage of the great gift of confession here and now, and get in a state of grace immediately. Delaying even one more minute is a death wish. St Alphonsus explains the importance (and beauty) of confession in the following way:

The priest has the power of … delivering sinners from Hell, of making them worthy of Paradise, and of changing them from the slaves of Satan into the children of God. And God Himself is obliged to abide by the judgment of His priests, and either not to pardon or to pardon, according as they refuse or give absolution, provided the penitent is capable of it.

More will be written on the death of a sinner later in this chapter.

The Calamity of Sin

Life is a lot like walking on a tightrope across a volcano. By sinning, we lose our balance to the left or to the right and fall into the fire. The Catholic Church teaches that one mortal sin, just one, merits eternal punishment. If we die in a state of mortal sin, without having made a perfect act of contrition, that's it. Game over. Nothing but a fiery hell awaits. Some might think that's quite harsh. Not St Alphonsus.

"The man who commits a mortal sin against God is like a heap of worms, who is so miserable and does not possess anything. Mortal sin is an act of infinite malice toward God," he affirms. "God is our last end," he continues. "When man prefers a vile pleasure to divine grace, he substitutes this last end with pleasure and makes pleasure his god! He is guilty of idolatry."

Every soul that loves God is loved by Him in return; and God dwells within it and leaves it not until He is expelled by sin. So, when the soul deliberately consents to mortal sin, it expels God, and as it were says to Him 'Leave me, O Lord for I desire to possess Thee no longer.'

The devil wants us to think sin isn't that big of a deal and that instead of walking on a wobbly rope over burning lava, life is more like strutting across a sturdy, two-foot wide beam of wood over a pool of water, and that there's no way we'll fall in. And even if we do, it'll be a soft landing due to God's mercy. St Alphonsus wholly rejects that way of thinking.

> In this life men walk in the midst of darkness, and in a slippery way. Hence, they are in danger of falling at every step, unless they cautiously examine the road on which they walk, and carefully avoid dangerous steps—that is, the occasion of sin.

Occasions of Sin

What are occasions of sin and why are they so dangerous? The saints are unanimous in teaching that there are two types of occasions of sin. One is avoidable while the other unavoidable.

Avoidable occasions of sin are situations that aren't obligatory for us to be in. Unavoidable occasions of sin are circumstances we can't escape regardless of our state in life.

St Alphonsus instructs Catholics to eliminate every avoidable occasion of sin. "In order to attain to loving God with all our heart, we must separate it from everything that is not God, that does not tend towards God." If we wish for Jesus Christ "to dwell within us, we must keep the doors of our senses closed again to dangerous occasions, otherwise the devil will make us his slaves." He elaborates on this point by stating: "He, then, who wishes to save his soul, must not only abandon sin, but also the occasions of sin: that is, he must renounce those wicked companions, and all similar occasions that incite him to sin."

What St Alphonsus is urging us to do here is to cut off those friends, places, forms of entertainment, and everything else that might lead us into sin. How can we do this?

After His resurrection, Jesus entered, though the doors were closed, to the upper room where the apostles were assembled. Aquinas says that, 'the Lord does not enter our souls unless we keep the door to our senses, and the temptations those senses arouse, shut.' We must, therefore, be on guard against all occasions of sin that tempt our senses. God withholds graces from those who voluntarily put themselves in occasions where temptation is.

Souls who think they can put themselves into occasions of sin and still resist it are fools, St Alphonsus further teaches. "It is impossible to stand amidst flames and not get burned at some point." When the soul "yields to the suggestions of the devil, and exposes herself to the occasions of sin, he easily enters and devours her. The ruin of our first parents arose from their not flying from the occasions of sin." All men must "resolve to remove the occasions of their faults; otherwise they will always relapse into the same defects."

For those who fail to remove occasions of sin in their lives, and fall back into their previous sinful lifestyle, St Alphonsus calls on them to earnestly beg the Lord to deliver them from this wretched state. We can by our own strength "do nothing," he reminds us, "but [we] can do all things with the assistance of God, who has promised to hear the prayers of all." Catholics must therefore "pray, and continue to pray without interruption. If we cease to pray, we shall be defeated; but if we persevere in prayer we shall conquer."

Breaking Free

All this talk about sin and occasions of sin reminds of the time I was trying to quit gambling. I was in my early thirties and built up a terrible addiction that began during my college years.

I was making decent money from my job and decided I had enough disposable income to go to the casino. I won. And lost. And won and lost. It was a vicious cycle that ultimately got the better of me.

I would tell myself I was going to quit, but the casino kept mailing me brochures informing me I had complimentary two-night stays at their hotel and $100 in free slot play. These occasions of sin kept tugging at me. "Just gamble for a few hours with what they gave you," I would say. "I'll only bring fifty dollars and if I lose it, I'll go home."

As you can imagine, things didn't turn out that way. I was, without a doubt, the textbook definition of what St Alphonsus calls a "tepid soul."

> A tepid soul is one that frequently falls into fully deliberate venial sins and does not have remorse for them ... the tepid soul is one who, like Peter, follows Christ but at a distance, a distance that they believe is safe and secure, and allows them one foot in both worlds: the natural and supernatural: without having to truly give oneself fully to Christ.

St Alphonsus explains that such souls are often allowed by God to fall into their miserable state of sin for a reason.

> God permits defects of this kind, even in the saints, to keep them humble, and to make them feel that, as they commit such faults in spite of all their good purposes and promises, so also, were they not supported by His divine hand, they would fall into mortal sins. Hence, when we find that we have committed these light faults, we must humble ourselves, and acknowledging our own weakness, we must be careful to recommend ourselves to God, and implore Him to preserve us, by His almighty hand, from

more grievous transgressions, and to deliver us from those we have committed.

My gambling addiction fit this description to a T. In fact, when I went to confession, the priest told me that God was likely pulling back His protective hand and letting me go on my way. He said God was testing me and probably wanted to let me fall in order to humble me and to remind me I can do nothing without Him. And to think that all this stemmed from a simple five-dollar poker game my freshman year of college. Be careful with the habits you develop in your youth. They can turn out to be major problems later in life.

The Danger of Venial Sins

No matter how hard we try to be perfect, all of us will falter at some point during our journey on this earth. "On account of the corruption of nature by Original Sin," St Alphonsus observes, "no man can be exempt from ... venial faults." This corruption "renders it impossible for us, without a most special grace, which has been given only to the Mother of God, to avoid all venial sins during our whole lives."

True as that is, we can't just throw up our arms in desperation. Either we pick ourselves up after each fall—just as Christ did on the road to Calvary—or we give into our sins by letting them overwhelm us with despair, which is what Judas Iscariot did by committing suicide after betraying Our Lord.

St Alphonsus clarifies that deliberate and habitual venial sins not only deprive us of strength to resist temptations, but also "of the special helps without which we fall into grievous sins." A great danger awaits, he says, for those who "commit many venial sins through attachment to any passion, such as pride, ambition, aversion to a neighbor, or an inordinate affection for any person."

Venial sins, it might be said, are similar to paper cuts. Of themselves—inadvertent ones in particular—they inflict a small amount of damage on our spiritual lives. If we care for them properly, they can heal rather quickly. But if we keep committing them, especially on purpose, we can find ourselves in a far more serious situation.

St Alphonsus affirms that repeated light faults lead souls into mortal sins. "Without feeling remorse" for "habitual and deliberate venial sins" we put ourselves in danger. "The fall of many souls into mortal sin follows from habitual venial sins; for these render the soul so weak, that, when a strong temptation assails her, she has not strength to resist it."

The devil is aware of all this. He wants to trip us up, and to trip us up badly. But he knows that it's difficult to get us to fall as fast and as hard as he wants us to in one fell swoop, so he seeks out our smallest faults and tries to create a snowball effect. On this point, St Alphonsus says the following. As you read it, think about some of the ways the devil tailors his approach to you and how he tries to get you to commit lesser sins that result in larger ones.

> St Francis of Assisi says that, in endeavoring to draw to sin a soul that is afraid of being in enmity with God, the devil does not seek in the beginning to bind her with the chain of a slave, by tempting her to commit mortal sin, because she would have a horror of yielding to mortal sin, and would guard herself against it. He first endeavors to bind her by a single hair; then by a slender thread; next by a cord; afterwards by a rope; and in the end by a chain of hell that is, by mortal sin; and thus he makes her his slave.

Temptations of the Devil

How many times has someone told you, "I'm a good person. I'm kind. I help strangers. And even though I don't go to church, I am spiritual. I don't think God—if there is a God—would ever send good people to Hell for eternity."

If you're like me, you hear this all the time. The truth is, it's one of the most naïve statements a person can make. Why? First off, we're born with Original Sin. This alone makes it extremely difficult to be "good" without the Sacraments. Second, being "good" isn't enough to merit Heaven. We have to be *holy* in order to obtain eternal life. "Without faith, it is impossible to please God," Hebrews 11:6 states. "Without Me, you can do nothing," Our Lord declares in John 15:5.

St Alphonsus echoes these sentiments by writing that "without the aid of grace we cannot do any good work, nor even think a good thought." He adds that "the power to avoid sin is not from ourselves but from the grace of God." He continues: "Without the aid of the Holy Ghost we cannot even pronounce the name of Jesus so as to deserve a reward."

When the devil sees a soul setting its sights on holiness, he springs into action. St Alphonsus says there are common tricks he uses to prevent souls from embracing the road to perfection.

First, he notes, the devil tells them they can go on sinning and that they will "eventually" get around to amending their life. This is false, St Alphonsus exclaims. "This postpones their conversion to God and not only delays but inevitably never makes them confess their sins." He goes on:

Imagine if you had a pearl in your hand and threw it in the river. Would you not dive after it right away? Your efforts later on may never allow you to find it. Like a thief in the night, death arrives at our doorstep. We need to always be watchful.

Second, the devil tells us that we have plenty of time to convert. In reality, "God counts not the years but the sins of individuals."

Third, Satan convinces us that we cannot resist sin, and that it's too difficult to not give in to it.

> The devil is making you think you do not have the grace to turn to God. It is too hard, the devil says! But this is foolish. God gives us enough grace to overcome the temptations we have. Indeed, God says to 'ask and it shall be given. Knock and it shall be opened.' The devil makes us think this is not true.

Fourth, Satan deceives souls into believing God will never send them to hell because of His mercy. "God is indeed merciful," St Alphonsus acknowledges, "but He is also just and He is obliged to punish those who offend Him without repentance."

Lastly, the devil tempts souls to think they can sin and still be saved based on the off-chance they will have done enough during their life to get into Heaven. "Indeed you may be saved," St Alphonsus tells his readers, "but there is also great reason to believe that by continually sinning you have merited eternal punishment." The obstinate sinner "will be cut off and thrown into the pit. Proverbs says, 'I called you but you refused. Therefore, I will laugh in your destruction and will mock you at the hour of death.'" That thought alone should motivate us to get right with God this very day!

Remedies to the Devil's Deceit

Here's a newsflash: even if we remove all avoidable occasions of sin, we'll still be tempted to sin. Why? Because it's part of God's plan that we prove our worth to Him during our time on earth. "God allows us to be tempted, to make us richer in merits, as Tobias was told: 'And because you were acceptable to God, it was necessary that temptation should prove you,'" St Alphonsus affirms. He offers the following advice when we're tempted to sin.

The first thing we should do, he says, is "have immediate recourse to God with all humility and confidence; saying: 'Incline unto my aid, O God, O Lord, make haste to help me!'" In temptations "against impurity, we should commit ourselves to not fight the temptation hand to hand, but to remove ourselves from the situation immediately." We should also "[apply] ourselves to some indifferent occupation calculated to distract us." St Alphonsus goes on:

> If the impure temptation has already forced its way into the mind, and plainly pictures its object to the imagination, so as to stir the passions, then, according to the advice of St Jerome, we must burst forth into these words: 'O Lord, thou art my helper.'

He continues:

> Should the temptation, however, obstinately persist in attacking us, let us beware of becoming troubled or angry at it; for this might put it in the power of our enemy to overcome us. We must, on such occasions, make an act of humble resignation to the will of God, who thinks fit to allow us to be tormented by these abominable temptations; and we must say: O Lord, I deserve to be molested with these filthy suggestions, in punishment of my past sins; but Thou must help to free me.

Another way the devil tempts us is by putting impure images on television. One easy way to avoid that is to either not own a TV at all or, if we do, when we're watching something and an immodest situation appears on the screen, simply turn it off. One method I've used that's been effective at combating impurity, particularly during conversations, is to share my opinion on something that changes the trajectory of the discussion altogether.

"Did you see that new music video by that pop star? Dang!"

"Yeah, what was she…"

"No, I didn't. I've been so busy working lately. I'm shocked she's still making albums. Hey, did you ever get that promotion?"

You can also re-direct a sinful conversation by bringing up someone's children, home remodeling, or any other generic topic. These might not be the most exciting things to discuss, but they can help minimize the spiritual damage done by sacrilegious dialogue. "He who loves God seeks to speak always of God," St Alphonsus reminds us.

St Alphonsus further suggests that when we're faced with temptations we can't escape, we should never cease calling on Jesus and Mary. The "most necessary, and the safest" remedy against temptation, he teaches, "is to have immediate recourse to God." He therefore advises that, "If you desire to possess … purity … you must cut off all dangerous occasions: you must cherish a holy ignorance of all that is opposed to chastity, and abstain from reading whatever has the slightest tendency to sully the soul."

St Alphonsus also draws our attention to the story of Adam and Eve as something we can learn from. "The ruin of our first parents arose from their not flying from the occasions of sin.… As long as we expose ourselves to the occasions of sin, the devil laughs at all our good purposes and promises made to God."

Conquering Common Sins

I'd like to spend a few moments talking about what St Alphonsus teaches about anger, impurity, bad friendships, crass language,

and human respect, as these are quite relevant for Catholics today. I'll then return to his warnings for those who delay their
conversion until death. After that, I'll conclude this book with
a final chapter on spiritual insights St Alphonsus provides that
are broader than the scope of these first six chapters.

"Anger resembles fire," St Alphonsus argues. "By the smoke
which it produces ... anger blinds us to see what is around us as
it engulfs us. It also chokes those around us and makes it impossible for others to be in its presence." He goes on:

> According to St Bonaventure, an angry man is incapable of
> distinguishing between what is just and what is unjust.....
> A man who does not restrain the impulse of anger, easily
> falls into hatred towards the person who has been the oc-
> casion of his passion.

How, then, do those who have a problem with anger overcome
it? By meekness and by imitating the Lamb of God! "Oh! how
pleasing in the sight of God are the meek, who submit in peace
to all crosses, misfortunes, persecutions, and injuries!" Catholics
on social media should most certainly heed this advice. St Alphonsus elaborates on this point by adding:

> We must be peaceful towards all men, even those who de-
> spise us. Bear patiently and with mercy the faults of oth-
> ers, just as God bears patiently and with mercy your own
> faults. The meekness of men is proved by humiliation. Thus,
> when we receive an insult, let us answer with meekness or
> remain silent ... if someone provokes you and you wish to
> fire back at them, you shall resort to the behavior of your
> enemy. This is not how Christ lived.

Regarding sins of impurity, St Alphonsus says that men will
always want more of them the more they indulge in them. Sins
of impurity "are not to be indulged even in the slightest," he

warns. "Some will say they can control it, but such a view is foolish." Impurity, "especially the impurity of the flesh … is the most vile offence." He continues: "Impurity of the body, such as drinking, also introduces chaos into us. It deprives us of our reason. God does not have patience for sins against impurity. Sodom and Gomorrah were destroyed for … impurity."

We must "always confess our sins against impurity and pray unceasingly to have the strength to overcome the temptation," he adds. One can only imagine what St Alphonsus would say about the proliferation of pornography on the Internet.

When it comes to bad friends and questionable acquaintances, St Alphonsus observes that we must never put human relationships before the truths of our faith.

> Nature inclines man to imitate what he sees other men do. If we have fellowship with the proud, we too will emulate their behavior. Scandalous friends and their actions poison your soul with their bad words, crass jokes and bad behaviors. These friends seek not your eternal welfare but temporary companions on the road to perdition. They want to be assured of their sinfulness by seeking your approval.

What can Catholics do to combat this temptation?

> We must avoid [bad friends] at all costs. Avoid their gatherings, their books, their type of entertainment. The devil employs vicious friends as decoys to draw us into the snares of sin. Seek to, when appropriate, reprove them so to convert them and show them the truth. If they became angry, it might as well be expected. When we are in a dark room and it is suddenly illuminated, doth not human nature incline us to throw up our hands to cover our eyes from the piercing brightness? Be patient and come back later on.

With regard to the way Catholics ought to talk, St Alphonsus warns that they must ever be on guard with their choice of words. "The tongue is like a spark in a fire." It "can cause the entire forest to be set ablaze if not controlled correctly. The spiritual tongue speaks of God. The worldly tongue speaks of this world and all its vanities, lies and impurities." The "wounds of a whip are but flesh deep," he adds. "The wounds of the obscene tongue infect the bones and the soul of those whom they are directed at."

St Alphonsus continues: "By using immodest language, you expose yourself to the proximate danger of falling into unchaste actions; for, according to St Jerome, as we have already said, 'he who delights in words, is not far from the act.'"

How, then, should Catholics speak?

You must weigh your words before you utter them ... when immodest words come to the tongue, you must suppress them; otherwise, by uttering them, you shall inflict on your own soul ... a mortal and incurable wound. God has given you the tongue, not to offend Him, but to praise Him and bless Him.... Reflect, says St Augustine, that your mouths are the mouths of Christians, which Jesus Christ has so often entered in the Holy Communion.... Our conversation should be seasoned with words calculated to excite others not to offend, but to love God ... avoid, as you would a plague, those who speak immodestly ... reprove with zeal the man who speaks obscenely.

Finally, when it comes to the temptation of human respect, St Alphonsus instructs us to be on guard as much as possible against befriending worldly individuals.

When we become friends with souls infected with the scandal of this world, we shall feel an unwillingness to oppose their bad practices and bad counsels. Thus, through fear of contradicting them, we imitate their example and lose friendship with God.

Catholics can steadfastly resist this temptation, he argues, by emulating St John the Baptist.

> To overcome human respect we must prefer the grace of God to all other goods and favors of this world. Expect to lose friends because of this. Indeed, how many of the apostles were at the foot of the cross when He was being sacrificed and going through His Passion? We must obey God, not the prince of this world. Let us imitate John the Baptist and upbraid those who need to be reproved and warn them of their worldly ways.

The Death of a Sinner

Earlier in this chapter I mentioned that St Alphonsus instructs souls not to wait until their death to confess their sins. I'd like to briefly highlight some of his remarks on that topic before moving on to Chapter 7.

St Alphonsus makes three main points regarding the death of a sinner. The first is that at the hour of death, the sinner will be tortured by remorse of conscience. Second, they will be tortured by assaults of the devil. Third, they will be assailed by the fear of eternal damnation.

Regarding the first point, St Alphonsus observes that initially the sinner will think his sickness is just another passing episode, and that he will overcome it just as he has all previous ones. But that is an illusion. "When his illness increases, and malignant symptoms ... begin to appear, then the storm with which the Lord has threatened the wicked shall commence." Then his sins will "rush upon his mind, and fill him with terror. His iniquities shall stand against him to convict him, and, without the aid of other testimony, shall assail him, and prove that he deserves hell."

Regarding the second point on which sinners face on their deathbed, St Alphonsus says they will be tormented by demons.

All his enemies will encompass him in the straits of death. One shall say: 'Be not afraid; you shall not die of this sickness!' Another will say: 'You have been for so many years deaf to the calls of God, and can you now expect that He will save you?' Another will ask: 'How can you repair the frauds of your past life, and the injuries you have done to your neighbor in his property and character?' Another shall ask: 'What hope can there be for you? Do you not see that all your confessions have been null that they have been made without true sorrow, and without a firm purpose of amendment? Do you not see that you are lost?' And in the midst of these straits and attacks of despair, the dying sinner, full of agitation and confusion, must pass into eternity.

Regarding the third point related to the death of a sinner, St Alphonsus states that it is true that, "in whatsoever hour the sinner is converted, God promises to pardon him; but to no sinner has God promised the grace of conversion at the hour of death." "It now justly belongs to me," the Lord will say to them, "to take vengeance on the insults you have offered me. You have despised my threats against obstinate sinners, and have paid no regard to them.... The time of my vengeance is now arrived; it is but just to execute it."

Avoid this terrible ending to your life, St Alphonsus exclaims. "While it is in your power, repent of all your past sins; for, a time shall come when you will be no longer able to avert the punishment which they deserve." Catholics need to take St Alphonsus' advice seriously and not put off any longer confessing their sins to a priest. Death comes when we least expect it.

The Death of a Saint

"The torments which afflict sinners at death, do not disturb the peace of the saint," St Alphonsus teaches. "The death of the Christian that loves God is called not death, but sleep."

Death is not always a pleasant subject to think about. We are, in many ways, socially conditioned to not reflect on it, and to focus instead on satisfying our material wants and bodily desires. But all men must leave this world behind. Such is the consequence of Original Sin. Death is merely the door we walk through to be born to eternal life. We should look at it, then, not with abject horror, as if it is the worst thing that could happen to us (falling into mortal sin is infinitely worse). Rather, we should look upon it, as St Alphonsus advises, with a sense of "joy and desire."

A chosen few Catholics today will, like those who lived in the first centuries of the Church, die as martyrs. Most, however, will likely pass away at home surrounded by friends and family. God hides from us the hour of our death so we will strive to remain in a state of grace.

In his book *Preparation for Death*, St Alphonsus encourages Christians to never forget that they are dust and that they are destined to be food for worms. Mere hours after death, the body starts to decay, repelling those around it with a foul odor, he says. Gone are its titles, wealth, possessions, and honors. Soon, no one will speak of it any longer. "In life he was the favorite," St Alphonsus writes, "now he makes all those who look upon him shudder." The pleasures the body experienced in life, which lasted but a moment, are gone forever, he continues. All that can be taken with it is its good deeds.

St Alphonsus himself could have stayed in the world and remained a successful lawyer. He also could have been married. Instead, he followed in the footsteps of Our Lord and laid down his life for others. "It was at the sight of death that the saints despised all the goods of this earth," he writes. "Labor in this life for the attainment of goods which are not lost at death."

A master of time management, St Alphonsus never wasted even a half hour of the day. His productivity was unequaled. The sheer volume of his writings alone is evidence of that. In his reflections on death, he urges Christians to not throw away what God has so lovingly given them. "Time is a treasure which is found only in this life." How ardently "shall we desire at death the time which we now squander away!" Every passing moment provides us with an opportunity to acquire "new treasures of eternal riches." "As St Ambrose tells us, the present life is given to us, not for repose, but that we may labor, and by our toils, merit eternal glory."

Catholics who pray the Rosary and are devoted to the Blessed Virgin Mary can be certain She will comfort them when their earthly journey nears its end, he additionally teaches. "The Divine Mother shall come to chase away the devils, and to protect Her servant." If at the hour of death "we have only the protection of Mary," St Alphonsus further remarks, "what need we fear from the whole of our infernal enemies?" "Take courage," he continues, "and have the confidence that Mary will come to assist us in death, and console us by her presence, if we serve and love her during the remainder of our life."

St Joseph, the patron saint of the dying, is also someone St Alphonsus encourages Christians to seek refuge in. "Since we all must die, we should cherish a special devotion to St Joseph, that he may obtain for us a happy death."

Final Perseverance

It is true that holy men and women have been tempted to despair in their final hours. St Thérèse of Lisieux experienced severe trials near the end of her life—as did St Alphonsus, who suffered from scrupulosity throughout his life. It's essential to recognize that these moments are nothing but the last-ditch efforts of an already defeated enemy meant to trick us into doubting the promises of Him who wishes to be with us for all eternity.

"Should the thought of having offended God at some part of our life molest us at death," St Alphonsus writes, "let us remember that … He forgets the iniquities of all penitent sinners." God "knows well how to console his children in their last moments; and, even in the midst of the pains of death, He infuses into their souls certain sweetnesses, as foretastes of paradise, which He will soon bestow upon them." At death, "the Lord shall wipe away from the eyes of his servants all the tears they have shed in this world."

One particular insight that St Alphonsus shares about the death of Our Lord has always stood out to me. It stands out because it serves as a direct rebuke to how the Western medical complex tends to operate. Consider, for example, how common it is for nurses or hospice workers to approach the family of a person who is near death to persuade them to administer drugs that will make them comfortable. St Alphonsus would have wholly rejected this practice.

> As soon as Jesus arrived on Calvary, oppressed with pain and fatigue, they gave him to drink wine mixed with gall, which was ordinarily given to persons condemned to the death of the cross, in order to diminish their sensibility to pain. But because Jesus wished to die without comfort, he tasted, but would not drink it.

St Alphonsus explains that, "he who dies loving God is not disturbed by the pains of death; but, seeing that he is now at the end of life, and that he has no more time to suffer for God, or to offer Him other proofs of his love, he accepts these pains with joy."

We should not fear death! When it arrives, we should approach it with the same sobriety and spiritual rigor we brought to every other trial we faced in life. We should use it, in other words, as an occasion to show God our love for Him. To spend our last waking hours tranquilized by numbing agents is the complete opposite of God's plan for us. If anything, those moments are gifts that, if fully embraced, will diminish our time in purgatory and even win graces for our loved ones here on earth.

Again, St Alphonsus advises Christians to offer the last hours of their life to God. Devout souls should unite "the sacrifice of [their own] death with the sacrifice which Jesus Christ offered for [them] on the cross," he teaches. A holy soul is "not afflicted at the thought of being obliged to take leave of the goods of the earth; for he has always kept his heart detached from them." St Alphonsus composed the following prayer for persons seeking the graces for a holy death:

My Lord Jesus Christ, by that bitterness which You endured on the Cross when Your soul was separated from Your sacred body, have pity on my sinful soul when it leaves my body to enter into eternity.

Mary, by that sorrow which thou experienced on Calvary, obtain for me a good death, that loving Jesus and you in this life, I may reach heaven where I shall love Thee both for all eternity. Amen.

Considerations

- Do I think about death every day? Am I truly living in such a way that if I died in the next 24 hours I would go to heaven? How can St Alphonsus' teachings better prepare me for my own death?

- Looking back at my life, how many sins have I committed in total? 1,000? 5,000? 50,000? How much is enough? I should go to confession immediately and thank God for being merciful to me, and for continually giving me chances to amend my life instead of sending me to hell.

- If my priest asked me what are the top three avoidable occasions of sin in my life right now, what would I tell him? Which of these can I remove from my life starting this week?

- What venial sins do I commit the most? Is it typical for me to fall into mortal sin soon afterwards? What people, places, or things can I surround myself with that will help me avoid venial (and mortal) sin?

- How does the devil usually tempt me? What seems to be his preferred method of attack? What advice does St Alphonsus provide that can help me combat his efforts to lead me into sin?

CHAPTER 7

SPIRITUAL WARFARE

Suppose you are, in fact, overcoming your dominant faults. That you're going to adoration, praying humbly (and continually) throughout the week, and not only joyfully embracing mortifications (and overcoming temptations to "bad self-love") but also removing all occasions of sin and worthily receiving—and thanking—God for the Eucharist. Will you, once you've done all this, find happiness? Will you, at that point, find favor with God? Actually, yes.

"God promises those who renounce their own will that He will raise them above the earth, and give them a celestial spirit," St Alphonsus teaches. "Whenever anyone desires nothing except what God desires" they acquire "that great peace which the saints experience." They come to possess "the freedom which the sons of God enjoy." Such a soul "does not only become a saint, but he enjoys, even in this world, perpetual peace."

At the same time, we mustn't think this life will only be filled with spiritual pleasures. "Love of God does not consist in experiencing His tenderness, but in serving Him with resolution and humility," St Alphonsus writes, citing St Teresa of Avila. "This earth is a place of merit which is acquired by suffering; Heaven is a place of reward and happiness."

Yours and my journey to perfection, our journey to unite our wills to God's Will, is going to include a lot of ups and downs.

Often times, you'll feel like giving up. Nevertheless, we must remain vigilant, and learn to not listen to our feelings but instead to discipline our will so that when we encounter difficulties we will remain faithful to God. "Desire nothing but what God desires. This is the sum and substance of that perfection to which we ought to aspire," St Alphonsus teaches. Job expressed something similar when he said, "The Lord giveth, and the Lord taketh away; blessed be the name of the Lord."[31]

What's important to remember during "the race" of our life is that there's actually a name for the desperation we feel when prayer is difficult and God seems far away. Those moments are called desolation, and they're not necessarily a bad thing, or, something you can't get out of.

"God's true lovers are discovered in times of aridity and temptation," St Alphonsus remarks, again citing St Teresa. "I am not saying that you will not suffer pain on seeing yourself bereft of the sensible presence of your God," he continues. "It is impossible for a soul not to feel such pain as this; nor can it refrain from lamentation."

When we experience desolation, it's easy to think God has forsaken us and that He's being cruel or unjust. St Alphonsus says that's the furthest thing from the truth. "Aridity keeps us diligent and humble, otherwise we become puffed up with spiritual pride and grow tepid, vainly believing we have reached the summit of sanctity." He continues:

> When you find yourself in aridity and darkness, so that you feel, as it were, incapable of making good acts, it is sufficient to say: 'My Jesus, mercy. Lord, for the sake of Thy mercy, assist me.' And the meditation made in this manner will be for you perhaps the most useful and fruitful.

31 Job 1:21

Everyone who ventures on the road to perfection goes through desolation at some point or another, almost always for different reasons and for different lengths of time. One Redemptorist priest I know told me he lived in spiritual darkness for more than two decades. A relative of mine experiences desolation every Lent. "The condition of the saints has been, ordinarily, one of dryness," St Alphonsus observes.

God also hides Himself from us during times of desolation because we've offended Him by sinning. Other times it's because He simply wants to remind us we can do nothing without Him. "Some foolish persons, seeing themselves in a state of aridity think that God may have abandoned them; or, again, that the spiritual life was not made for them; and so they leave off prayer, and lose all that they have gained," St Alphonsus comments. In truth, "there is no time better for exercising our resignation to the will of God than that of dryness." He goes on:

> Although sometimes, when we are in a state of aridity, or disturbed by some fault we have committed, we perhaps do not feel while praying that sensible confidence which we would wish to experience, yet, for all this, let us force ourselves to pray; and to pray without ceasing; for God will not neglect to hear us. Nay, rather He will hear us more readily; because we shall then pray with more distrust of ourselves; and confiding only in the goodness and faithfulness of God, who has promised to hear the man who prays to Him. Oh, how God is pleased in the time of our tribulations, of our fears, and of our temptations, to see us hope against hope; that is, in spite of the feeling of diffidence which we then experience because of our desolation!

What else should Catholics do when they are experiencing dryness and desolation? One thing they can do is meditate. "Happy is he who does not leave off meditation in the hour of desolation," St Alphonsus writes. Another thing they can do is receive the Eucharist. "When you are tepid, you should more frequently approach [Holy Communion]." "As St John Avila used to say, one 'Blessed be God' in times of adversity, is worth more than a thousand acts of gratitude in times of prosperity." More will be said about desolation in a moment.

Consolation

The opposite of desolation is consolation. Consolation occurs when, among other things, it is easy to pray, enjoyable to go to adoration, and pleasing to meditate. We simply find comfort in all things related to the spiritual life. "I call consolation every increase of hope, faith and charity, and all interior joy which calls and attracts to heavenly things and to the salvation of one's soul, quieting it and giving it peace in its Creator and Lord," St Ignatius of Loyola once said.[32]

Several years ago, the priest at my chapel gave a memorable sermon wherein he compared consolation to candy. When we are children, all we want is candy, he said. It satisfies our sweet tooth. We *feel* good when we have it. The only problem is, you can't develop a healthy body on candy alone. There's no nutritional value in it. Plus, we eventually crash from the sugar rush. In order to properly develop, we need to have it taken away from us. Any good parent will do this—so, too, will God, who wants us to become saints. He gives us consolations once in a while to help us, but He takes them away so we can advance spiritually and prove to Him we love Him for His own sake, and not that we love the consolations themselves.

32 Ludovic-Marie Barrielle, *Rules for Discerning Spirits: In the Spiritual Exercises of St Ignatius of Loyola* (Kansas City, MO: Angelus Press, 1995).

When we are sent consolations and desolations, the saints advise that we should remain steadfast in our prayer life. "How many people, for all their efforts to study hard and acquire learning, become neither holy nor learned, because true learning is the knowledge of the saints, that is, learning how to love Jesus Christ," St Alphonsus points out. If we're given a consolation, we should thank God for His generosity. If we're given desolations, we should remind ourselves of what James 1:3 says: "Blessed is the man that endures temptation; for when he hath been proved, he shall receive a crown of life, which God hath promised to them that love Him."

Tribulations

When I went on my five-day silent retreat in 2018, I experienced all the desolation and consolation a soul can have in a single week. As already mentioned in Chapter 3, on the last day of my retreat I was rewarded with an intense spiritual experience that I'll treasure for the rest of my life. But the week itself was not easy. I was having terrible neurological symptoms the entire time, which made prayer extremely difficult. In fact, on the day of my arrival, I took a bite of a ham and cheese sandwich and instantly had a massive reaction that spread to all of my extremities for several hours. It was so bad that I only slept three hours that night.

Two days into the retreat, I was tempted to give up. "I'm too sick for this! Why did I even come? I'll just come back another time. This was a huge mistake," I told myself. "Tomorrow, I'll talk with Father to let him know I'm leaving early. I tried to serve You, Lord, but You've decided to make me suffer instead!"

Before heading to the priest's chambers to inform him of my plan, I went to the chapel to meditate. I sat, and listened, with no particular goal in mind. Slowly, my soul began to stir. By the grace of God, I came to realize how absurd it would've been for me to leave. The retreat house was in Connecticut. I lived in Michigan. I'd driven there over the previous two nights, stopping for a stay with a friendly Catholic family in Pittsburgh. I was a full 16-hour drive from home. Even if I wanted to leave, it wouldn't have been possible to get back in time to treat my symptoms. On top of that, none of the supplements I'd been taking were improving my illness anyway. It would have been a complete waste of time.

Looking back, this sort of irrational thinking is precisely what the devil wants us to do during times of tribulation. He wanted me to not use common sense. He wanted me to do something totally illogical and against what basic reason says to do.

Now, some might think that God was cruelly punishing me with these spiritual assaults. Not so, affirms St Alphonsus. "The man whom the Lord afflicts in this life has a certain proof that he is dear to God." He explains:

> The Lord sends [tribulations] to us, not because He wishes our misfortune, but because He desires our welfare. Hence, when they come upon us, we must embrace them with thanksgiving, and must not only resign ourselves to the Divine Will, but must also rejoice that God treats us as He treated His Son Jesus Christ, whose life upon this Earth was always full of tribulation.

Benefits of Tribulations

St Alphonsus teaches that there are several advantages to tribulations, and that they're not arbitrary punishments meant for God's enjoyment, but actually forms of spiritual medicine meant to help us on our journey to Heaven.

The first advantage of tribulations, he says, is they open the eyes of our souls to the true state it's in that prosperity had previously closed.

> St Paul remained blind after Jesus Christ appeared to him, and, during his blindness, he perceived the errors in which he had lived. During his imprisonment in Babylon, King Manasses had recourse to God, was convinced of the malice of his sins, and did penance for them.

Second, tribulations take from our heart all affections we have for earthly things.

> When a mother wishes to wean her infant, she puts gall on the paps, to excite his disgust.... God treats us in a similar manner: to detach us from temporal goods, He mingles them with gall, that by tasting their bitterness, we may conceive a dislike for them, and place our affections on the things of Heaven.

This precise scenario happened to me on my own spiritual journey in my early thirties. As already mentioned in Chapter 3, the pop music I used to listen to on my car radio was no longer meaningful after I started reading St Alphonsus. But I also became better at putting sports into their proper place. When I was in high school and college, I, like a lot of young American men, religiously watched Notre Dame football on Saturday and professional golf on Sunday. I also obsessed over the Detroit Tigers baseball team. I would even binge-watch television shows like *Seinfeld* and *The Office*. St Alphonsus helped free me from those empty forms of entertainment. "Those who truly love Jesus Christ lose all affection for worldly goods," he explains. Not being chained to those time-consuming, meaningless competitions and crass programs has allowed me to focus on other, more edifying behaviors instead.

A third benefit of tribulations, St Alphonsus teaches, is that they free us from pride, vainglory, and a desire for worldly goods. Tribulations "make us humble and content in the state in which the Lord places us." They help us place our "trust in God alone, and not in created things."

Fourth, tribulations give us the chance to atone for our past sins. "Job called those happy whom God corrects by tribulations; because He heals them with the very hands with which He strikes and wounds them."

Fifth, tribulations remind us that God alone can relieve us of our miseries.

Sixth, tribulations are opportunities to exercise the virtues of humility, patience, and resignation to God's Will. On this subject, St Alphonsus makes the following point:

> When we see a sinner in tribulation in this life, we may infer that God wishes to have mercy on him in the next and that he exchanges eternal for temporal punishment. But miserable is the sinner who the Lord does not punish in this life. For those whom He does not chastise … He reserves eternal chastisement.

Lukewarmness

It's easy to lose hope when we experience tribulations. Oftentimes what souls do when God isn't there to console them is to indulge in the things they found comfort in before He entered their life. "As a dog that returns to his vomit, so is the fool that repeats his folly," Proverbs 26:11 says. In other words, they revert to vices like excessive alcohol consumption or other sins like impurity and gluttony. These are reliable comforts in that they make us feel a certain way every time we use them. God, on the other hand, is less predictable.

In reality, these empty pleasures are nothing more than illusions that won't give us what we truly need. "Souls of little faith," St Alphonsus remarks, "instead of turning to God in their tribulations, have recourse to human means, and thus provoke God's anger, and remain in their miseries."

When we're tempted to turn our back on God and indulge in the things the world has to offer, we must recognize the importance of turning to Him all the more. "We should ... pray to [God], and never cease to pray until He hears us," St Alphonsus advises. We must "abandon sin, and endeavor to recover the grace of God."

St Ignatius of Loyola, a spiritual master like St Alphonsus, likewise recommends that in times of lukewarmness and tribulations that we re-double our efforts to recover the zeal we had before.

> Be firm and constant in the resolutions and determination in which one was the day preceding such desolation, or in the determination in which he was in the preceding consolation. Because, as in consolation it is rather the good spirit who guides and counsels us, so in desolation it is the bad, with whose counsels we cannot take a course to decide rightly.[33]

Reasons for Lukewarmness

As mentioned in Chapter 6, St Alphonsus teaches that venial and mortal sins can cause us to be lukewarm. He further observes that there are two types of lukewarmness—one is unavoidable while the other is avoidable.

33 Robert McTeigue, "Resist! It is time to rally against the darkness," Aleteia. org, 9 Sep 2017, https://aleteia.org/2017/09/13/resist-its-time-to-rally-against-the-darkness/#.

Regarding unavoidable lukewarmness, "the saints are not even exempt." This happens "as a result of our natural frailty" when we're sometimes distracted during prayer and when we fall victim to "useless words" and vain curiosities. Avoidable lukewarmness occurs when a person commits deliberate venial faults. This happens when we intentionally daydream during prayer or when we offer "little detractions, imprecations, expressions of anger, derisions of one's neighbor, [and] cutting words."

St Alphonsus urges us to tremble at the thought of committing a deliberate fault, for they "cause God to close His hands from bestowing upon us His clearer lights and stronger helps." He also says that if the lukewarmness we're experiencing is indeed a punishment for our sins, we should accept it by uniting ourselves to God's Will. "We merit hell for our sins. We should be consoled that God chastises us in this life."

Overcoming Lukewarmness

No one wants to be lukewarm forever. And neither does God want us to be. According to St Alphonsus, there are several ways we can overcome lukewarmness.

First, we should recommit ourselves to perfectly uniting ourselves to God's Will. "God wishes all to be saints and each one according to his state of life.... Courageous souls make considerable progress in a short period of time."

Second, we should make a firm resolution to actually attain perfection.

Many are called to perfection ... but because they never really resolve to acquire it, they live and die in the ill-odor of their tepid and imperfect life.... The slothful man is ever desiring, but never resolves to take the means suitable to his state of life to become a saint. He says: 'Oh, if I could but go and reside in another monastery, I would give my-self entirely up to God'.... Such desires do more harm than good.... We must ... desire perfection, and resolutely take the means towards it ... and to die rather than commit any deliberate sin whatever, however small it may be.

Third, we must have recourse to prayer to overcome luke-warmness. Prayer is a "blessed furnace in which the fire of holy love is enkindled and kept alive." St Alphonsus goes on:

We ought to be resigned in times of spiritual desolation. The Lord is accustomed, when a soul gives itself up to the spiritual life, to heap consolations upon it, in order to wean it from the pleasures of the world; but afterwards, when He sees it more settled in spiritual ways, He draws back His hand, in order to make proof of its love, and to see wheth-er it serves and loves Him unrecompensed, while in this world, with spiritual joys.

Lastly, if we wish to overcome lukewarmness, we should re-ceive Holy Communion:

They who Communicate most frequently are further ad-vanced in perfection.... St Bernard asserts that Communion represses anger and incontinence.... St John Chrysostom says, that Communion pours into our souls a great incli-nation toward virtue, and a promptitude to practice it.

Hope

After reading St Alphonsus, it might be easy to think that it's downright impossible to get into Heaven. The sheer depth and magnitude of his writings can make you feel overwhelmed with near-impossible expectations of holiness.

I can't tell you how many sleepless nights I had during my early thirties when my health was at its worst and I thought I was going to die. In those moments, I would despair over the sins I committed in my life. I would just lie there in absolute terror of my impending judgment—despite not being in a state of mortal sin—thinking to myself there is simply no way God is going to say to me if I died, "Well done good and faithful servant. Come, inherit the Kingdom prepared for you that was set forth from the foundations of the world."

Before encountering St Alphonsus, I considered hope to be the most confusing of the three theological virtues. The other two—faith and charity—were fairly straightforward. But hope was always difficult to grasp. I complained about that to a friend of mine several years ago. "God could kill me at any second. What is there to 'hope' for? I could live a holy life for sixty years, commit one mortal sin, and God is going to punish me with eternal suffering right then and there? Why should I have 'hope' that I'll be spared? What's the point? It's all a matter of free will!"

In his writings, St Alphonsus clarifies that Christian hope rests on the unshakable promises of God Himself and that "he that hopes in the Lord shall be encompassed by His mercy." He further points out that although we are deserving of punishment, "Jesus is far more powerful to win God's love for us than we are to draw down His hatred on ourselves, for God loves His Divine Son more than He hates the sinner." St Alphonsus explains this point in the following way:

> We must act as if the obtaining of our salvation depended entirely on ourselves, and yet we must place all our confidence in God and be thoroughly convinced that of ourselves we are utterly unable to attain what we desire. God accomplished everything by means of His grace, but He nevertheless desires our cooperation. If this cooperation,

insignificant though it is, be wanting, God withdraws from us and treats us as indolent servants deserving of naught but to be cast out into exterior darkness.

Again, it's true that God is a just God, and, as St Alphonsus repeatedly teaches, sin is a great offense to Him, even venial sin. But God is also patient and merciful. He desires that all men be saved. "My delights are to be with the children of men," Proverbs 8:31 reminds us. Catholics need to know that God will reward them if they continually put themselves back into His loving hands after falling into sin. "To every sinner who desires to repent, He promises pardon," St Alphonsus recalls. "Why are you tortured with fear and distrust?" he further asks. "Reanimate your courage at the sight of so many saints who lived for a long time at enmity with God, but returned to Him repentant and sorry."

When all is said and done, God is not a thunderbolt-throwing tyrant waiting around, laying traps for us to slip up so He can punish us for all eternity. Nor is He a nice old man in the clouds who lets anybody into Heaven. Christ purchased us with His Blood by suffering a horrific death for us. There is no clearer sign that He loves us and wants us to spend eternity with Him. Life is a gift, and God, who never stops loving us, wants to forgive us and to see us follow in Christ's footsteps. Hope allows us to know this and to live joyfully while trusting in God's loving promises.

The Blessed Virgin Mary

No book that presents the teachings of St Alphonsus would be complete without mentioning his writings on Mary, the Mother of God. One of the chief Mariologists in Church history, St Alphonsus was deeply devoted to the Blessed Virgin, and for good reason. She appeared to him on multiple occasions—several times when he sought spiritual refuge in a cave near Scala as a young priest; again when he was in Foggia in 1732 preaching a novena on her; and later, when he was giving a sermon in 1745, during which he levitated several inches off the ground.

As was mentioned in this book's Introduction, it was at Mary's altar in the Church of Our Lady of Ransom where Alphonsus vowed to become a priest. Throughout his life, he fasted on Saturdays in her honor and instructed his priests to preach about her during their missions. "No sermon is more profitable, or produces so much compunction in the hearts of the people, as the one on the mercy of Mary," he has said.

In the 1860s, Blessed Pope Pius ix entrusted to the Redemptorist Order the Icon of Our Lady of Perpetual Help, which currently resides at the Church of St Alphonsus in Rome. Although Catholics should already have a certain level of knowledge about Mary, St Alphonsus' writings will help them grow in love and appreciation for her as our advocate with Christ.

In his 600+ page book *Glories of Mary* (which is still widely regarded as one of the definitive guides to Catholic teaching on Mary), St Alphonsus presents, in painstaking detail, Biblical as well as traditional arguments in her defense. Those who read it will enjoy, among other things, a line-by-line analysis of the *Salve Regina* prayer as well as a thorough examination of all aspects of her life, beginning with her Immaculate Conception, her time spent in the Temple as a child, the Annunciation, and her sharing in Christ's passion and death. He also presents prayers that various saints composed to Mary and provides what can only be called a Holy Spirit-inspired analysis of her chief virtues. It would not be difficult to write an entire chapter on what St Alphonsus teaches about Mary. At the same time, like so many other parts of this book, an abridged presentation will have to suffice.

Queen of Mercy

St Alphonsus observes that the very name of Mary is of divine origin. "This name came not of earth, but from heaven." After the name of Jesus, "the name of Mary is above every other name." It has "the power to overcome the temptations of hell."

While Protestants often belittle—even ridicule—Mary's role in salvation history, St Alphonsus reasons that due to the fact that Christ is King of the Universe, Mary must be its queen. "From the moment that Mary consented to become the mother of the Eternal Word she merited the title of queen of the world and of all creatures." But what sort of queen is she? She is not a queen of justice, one who is intent upon the punishment of the guilty, for that is Christ's domain. Rather, Mary is "the queen of mercy, solely intent upon compassion and pardon for sinners." If "because of our sins we fear to draw near to God because He is an infinite Majesty that we have offended, we should not hesitate to have recourse to Mary, because in her we shall find nothing to alarm us."

Many non-Catholics like to point out that Christ declared in the Gospel of John that "no one comes to the Father except through me."[34] They conclude that it's blasphemous to ask for Mary's assistance. What these poor souls forget is that Mary is not our intercessor with *God the Father* but instead with *God's (and her) Son*, Jesus Christ. "There is no doubt, says St Bernard, that Jesus is the only Mediator of justice between God and man," St Alphonsus admits. "But because men recognize and fear in Jesus Christ the divine majesty ... it was necessary that another advocate should be assigned to us, to whom we could then have recourse with less fear and more confidence; and this is Mary." As "the Son intercedes for us with the Father, thus [Mary] intercedes for us with the Son."

34 John 4: 6

St Alphonsus points to the Miracle at the Wedding Feast of Cana as an example of Mary's unique influence with Our Lord. "Jesus Christ, indeed to please His mother, changed the water into the best wine." St Thomas Aquinas, he also writes, affirms that "Christ wished to show that He would have deferred the miracle, if another had asked Him to perform it; but because His mother asked it, He immediately performed it." The Son "denies nothing that the Mother asks," St Alphonsus concludes.

It should be noted that in obeying Mary's request at Cana, Our Lord was purposefully granting her the privilege of commencing His ministry, as He had not yet performed a public miracle. *She*, in other words, is responsible for having put *Him* on the road to Calvary, where He offered Himself for our redemption. It is, therefore, *at her intervention* that our salvation was secured. "If Jesus is the father of our souls, Mary is the mother," St Alphonsus writes. "For, in giving us Jesus, she gave us the true life; and offering upon Calvary the life of her Son for our salvation, she then brought us forth to the life of divine grace."

Mary's ability to obtain whatever she seeks from God should give us reason to have hope in her. "The Son has so great a regard for the prayers of Mary," St Alphonsus observes while referencing the writings of St Peter Damian, "that when she prays, she seems to command rather than request." Mary, who is now in heaven, body and soul, is closer to God than any other person who lived. She "never committed any sin or the slightest imperfection," St Alphonsus recalls. As a result, she "sees no one above her but her Son." This proximity grants her the special privilege of pleading our case with Christ more effectively than anyone else.

There are countless stories of persons who have either turned their lives around after praying the Rosary or, who, after having lived a sin-filled life, were spared eternity in hell because of the miraculous aid of this merciful mother. This is because Mary, who was the Mother of the Savior of mankind during her earthly life, is, by extension, also the mother of mankind itself. "Jesus was her first-born according to the flesh, but men were her second-born according to the spirit," St Alphonsus maintains. When Christ said to St John from the Cross to behold his mother, "Mary was then made [not only his] mother ... but [mother] of all men." Like any good mother, she tirelessly seeks what is best for us.

The Immaculate Conception

St Alphonsus died at noon on August 1, 1787, just as the Angelus was being prayed. No clearer sign could have been given to indicate he was greatly loved by our Blessed Mother. "Let us always beseech [Mary] to obtain for us a happy death," he advised. "Let us beg her to obtain the grace to die on a Saturday, which is a day dedicated in her honor."

Mary is no ordinary woman. In her womb lived the Savior of Mankind. "Who has loved God more than Mary?" St Alphonsus asks. She was, he reasons, the new Ark of the Covenant. Seeing how it would not have been appropriate for God, who is all-perfect, to physically dwell in that which is imperfect, Mary would have been created, by necessity, free from sin. "How can we think that the Son of God would have chosen to inhabit the soul and body of Mary without first sanctifying her and preserving her from every sin?" St Alphonsus wonders. "It was fitting that God should preserve her from Original Sin, since she was destined to stand in opposition to the devil." He continues: "St Cyril of Alexandria asks ... Who has ever heard of an architect building a house for his own use and then giving the first possession of it to his greatest enemy?" The tree is known by its fruit, he continues. "If the Lamb was always immaculate, the Mother must also have been always immaculate."

St Alphonsus' staunch defense of Mary's Immaculate Conception—which he was making a full century before it was declared a dogma of the faith in 1854—is firmly rooted in Scripture. "Blessed art thou among women," St Elizabeth declares in the Gospel of Luke, an obvious reference to Mary's favored status.[35] "Hail, full of grace, the Lord is with thee," the Archangel Gabriel proclaimed at the Annunciation.[36] No heavenly being has ever uttered such words to a mere creature!

Commenting on the meaning of these messages, St Alphonsus explains that by accepting to be the vessel—"the aqueduct," as he calls her—that would bring Jesus Christ, grace incarnate, into the world, Mary was made "the universal channel ... through which all the other graces which Our Lord is pleased to dispense to us should pass." No creature "has received any grace from God except by the intervention and hand of Mary," he teaches.

Speaking analogously, St Alphonsus compares Mary to the neck of the Mystical Body of Christ, which has Jesus at its head. He also refers to her as the moon, which, in reflecting the brightness of the sun, is not as severe in its illumination but still serves as a guide for those who "blindly wander in the night of sin." Sinners who have "lost the light of the sun, by losing divine grace" should "turn to the moon, [and] pray to Mary."

St Alphonsus' comparison of Mary to the moon is especially helpful in that it drives home the point that she is not perfection itself, but nonetheless resides above all other heavenly beings, second only to the Trinity. He himself makes note of this by observing that "the dignity of [the] Mother of God is the greatest dignity that can be conferred on a pure creature." This "divine Mother is infinitely inferior to God, but immensely superior to all creatures," for, without her consent, the Incarnation, and thus, the redemption of mankind, could not have occurred.

35 Luke 1:42   36 Luke 1: 26–28

Mary's Divine Protection

Mary loves us. And just as she was there when Jesus fell on the road to Calvary, she will also be there to help us when *we* fall into sin on our own journey to heaven. "She has a heart so kind and compassionate ... that she cannot send away dissatisfied any one who invokes her aid," St Alphonsus teaches.

But if we wish to remain in her good favor, and obtain what we ask for, we must first turn away from our bad habits. "Mary is the mother of sinners who desire to be converted," St Alphonsus recalls. While it is true that she "has desired the salvation of all," she "cannot love" the "obstinate" sinner. Therefore, "whoever aspires to be the son of this great mother, must first leave off sinning, and then let him hope to be accepted as her son." The "sons of Mary ... are her imitators in chastity, humility, meekness, mercy."

Unlike Lucifer, when Mary learned of her elevated status, her response was not one of pride or self-glorification. Instead, it was one of profound humility. "Behold the handmaid of the Lord. Be it done unto me according to Thy word," she said in response to Archangel Gabriel.[37] St Alphonsus explains that these words indicate Mary's desire to praise "the infinite greatness and goodness of God" while admitting "her own nothingness." The "higher she saw herself raised, the more she humbled herself," he teaches.

What can you and I do to place ourselves under this merciful mother's protection? And how can we ensure that she will be our advocate in this life and at our judgment in the next? According to St Alphonsus, those who love Mary engage in a variety of charitable acts. "Clients of the Blessed Virgin are accustomed to give alms to the poor in honor of the Divine Mother, especially on Saturdays." They honor her further by praying three Hail

37 Luke 1:38

Marys in the morning and at night, and by fasting on bread and water on Saturdays and on the vigils of her feasts. There are "innumerable favors" that she grants to those who also visit her in her churches and venerate her images, he adds. Strive also, he instructs, to read books on her and to request favors from her as often as possible. "If I did not pray my rosary for even one day, I would fear for my eternal salvation," he once remarked. "If you love Mary, endeavor to induce others to love her." To be devoted to Mary is "a mark of predestination."

Mother of Priests

Before concluding this section on Mary, it's worth drawing attention to additional comments St Alphonsus has made on her role in the life of religious, for they, he argues, are especially loved by her.

In remarks directed to young men considering the priesthood, St Alphonsus advises that they should not neglect, even for a single day, visiting the Blessed Sacrament and conversing with Our Lady. Doing this will ensure that they obtain the grace of perseverance. He also recalls that St Phillip Neri considered Mary his "delight" and that St Bonaventure referred to her as "his lady and mother ... [and] his heart and his soul."

On a sheer logical level, there is no better soul for priests (as well as laity) to turn to than Mary to stay close to Christ. When Our Lord was a boy, Mary and Joseph lost Him for three days. They eventually found Him preaching in the temple. As such, Mary, more than anyone else, knows what it's like to lose contact with Our Lord, which is what happens when we sin. If we wish to recover our relationship with God, let us seek her first. On this point, St Alphonsus provides the following story:

St Francis Borgia always doubted the perseverance of those in whom he did not find particular devotion to the Blessed Virgin. On one occasion he questioned some novices as to the saints towards whom they had special devotion, and perceiving some who had it not towards Mary, he instantly warned the master of novices, and desired him to keep a more attentive watch over these unfortunate young men, who all, as he had feared, lost their vocations and renounced the religious state.

Nuns and sisters can also look to Mary as an example. "Examine whether you will be more happy in having for your spouse a man of this world, or Jesus Christ, the Son of God and the King of heaven," St Alphonsus wrote to a woman considering religious life. "If Jesus Christ has called you to His love, and wishes to have you for His spouse, go on joyfully."

Virgins are especially dear to Jesus and Mary, he also argues. "The Mother of God once said to a soul, that a spouse of Jesus Christ ought to have great esteem for all virtues, but that purity, by which she is principally assimilated to her divine spouse, should hold the first place in her heart." Religious virgins "are, in the first place, as dear to God as His angels."

Priests and women religious should therefore eagerly solicit the help of Mary in their ministry. "This Son of God, the servant of the Father ... made Himself ... the servant of His creatures, Mary and Joseph," St Alphonsus observes. Jesus was "pleased to ... make himself subject to Mary." If Christ submitted himself to Mary, clergy should as well. Below is a brief prayer St Alphonsus composed to our Blessed Mother to help us remain close to her.

Most holy immaculate Virgin Mary, my Mother, I, most miserable of sinners, kneel before thee, the advocate, the hope, and the refuge of sinners. I venerate thee great queen, and I thank thee for the many favors thou hast already obtained for me, especially for having saved me from Hell which I have so often deserved.

I love thee, most amiable Lady, worthy of all love. And because I love thee, I promise to serve thee always, and to do everything in my power to make others serve thee also. In thee I hope; I place my salvation in thy hands.

Accept me for thy servant; receive me under thy mantle, Mother of Mercy. Thou art all-powerful with God. Free me, then, from all temptations, or at least obtain for me the strength to conquer them as long as I live.

From thee I seek a genuine love of Jesus Christ. With thy help I hope to die a good death. I beseech thee, Mother, to help me always, but especially at the last moment of my life. Do not leave me until you see me safe in heaven, blessing thee and singing thy mercies for all eternity. Amen.

The following hymn, composed by St Alphonsus to Mary for protection from the devil, can also help souls seek refuge under her maternal care.

> Haste, my Mother, run to help me;
> Mother, haste, do not delay;
> See from hell the envious serpent
> Comes my trembling soul to slay.
>
> Ah! his very look affrights me,
> And his cruel rage I fear;
> Whither fly, if he attacks me?
> See him, see him coming near!
>
> Lo! I faint away with terror,
> For if yet thou dost delay,

He will dart at me his venom;
Then, alas! I am his prey.

Cries and tears have nought availed me,
Spite of all I see him there;
Saints I call till I am weary,
Still he stands with threatening air.

Now his mighty jaws are open,
And his forked tongue I see;
Ah! He coils to spring upon me—
Mother! Hasten, make him flee.

Mary! Yes, the name of Mary
Strikes with dread my cruel foe;
Straight he flees as from the sunbeam
Swiftly melts the winter's snow.

Now he is gone, but do thou ever
Stay beside me, Mother dear;
Then the hellish fiend to tempt me
Nevermore will venture near.

The Road to Heaven

Ultimately, how is it we can know we are on the road to perfection (and heaven)? Are there ways we can be sure we're actually doing what God wants us to do? Yes, St Alphonsus says, there are two primary signs by which we can be confident we are doing God's Will.

The first indication we're doing God's Will is that we're obeying His teachings. "If we always act for God, according to His commands," and "overcome everything that is contrary to our nature for God, then we have the love of God in us." The second way we can know we're doing God's Will is if we're offering up our sufferings for Him. If we have patience and are "willingly suffering everything for Him," we have the love of God in us. St Alphonsus continues:

> When Jesus was going to His Passion, we can see that He loved God. This is the surest sign of love of God: willing to endure anything and to suffer anything for Him. This is what the holy martyrs exhibited when they died for Our Lord.

At the end of the day, there are only two options for us in this brief life. We either say to God, echoing the words of Mary, "Do unto me according to thy word," or we reject God's Will and say, repeating the words of the devil, "I will not serve!" There is no middle road. "We must suffer, and all must suffer," St Alphonsus declares. "Each one must carry his cross. He that carries it with patience is saved, he that carries it with impatience is lost." This is our only choice, to take up our cross and unite ourselves with Christ's Passion, or reject it and leave off our salvation! As Scripture reminds us, "the servant is not greater than his Lord."[38]

In Chapter 1, it was mentioned that St Alphonsus defines perfection as uniting ourselves with God. Perfection is "founded entirely on the love of God." "Perfect love of God ... consists in uniting" our will with God's Will. The more one "unites his will with the Divine Will ... the greater his love of God will be."

St Alphonsus asks us to reflect on the following questions: Do we always work for God's glory? Do we have an intention of doing everything for Him? Do we voluntarily suffer poverty, sickness, and tribulations for His sake? Do we, when tribulations come upon us, offer them to the Lord with promptness? If we respond "yes" to all these questions, St Alphonsus says

38 John 13:16

we have the love of God in us and can be assured that we are on the road to heaven.

Considerations

- Do I leave off prayer when I am desolate? Do I cling to consolations? Or do I praise God even when I don't want to, knowing that He deserves to be glorified no matter how I feel?

- How can I benefit from the tribulations I am going through right now? What lessons does God want me to take away from them?

- When I am lukewarm, do I give up hope and fall further into sin or do I persevere and remain confident in God's promises? How can I apply to my own life St Alphonsus' advice for those who are lukewarm?

- Have I prayed the Rosary today? How can I grow closer to Mary? What does St Alphonsus teach about her that I can introduce into my spiritual life right away?

- What are five things I can do over the next week, month, and year to grow in perfection by uniting my will with God's Will?

EPILOGUE

I've spent the entirety of this book explaining what St Alphonsus teaches about uniting our will to God's Will. It is important to never forget that Christ Himself has also told us how we can do this.

In the Gospel of John, Our Lord says, "If you love me, keep my commands."[39] In the Gospel of Matthew, he tells the rich man: "If thou wishes to be perfect, go and sell all that you have and give it to the poor, and then come follow me."[40]

Christ wants us to give ourselves entirely to Him. He wants us to incorporate our faith into everything we do, and to adhere to the many teachings of the Catholic Church. Yet for many Catholics, confessing sins to a priest, not admitting women to the priesthood, and banning pre-marital sex are just some of the "rules and regulations" they consider to be arbitrary dictates imposed on them by hypocritical old men.

Protestants also like to claim that Jesus didn't leave behind a Church with a pope at its head. "The Bible interprets itself. I do not need a priest. God will forgive my sins! By faith alone I am saved," one often hears.

The simplest response to these popular, though erroneous, arguments is that the doctrines of the Catholic Church are directly inspired by the Holy Spirit. "When the Spirit of truth comes," Christ said to His apostles as He ascended into Heaven,

39 John 14:15   40 Matthew 19: 21

"He will guide you."[41] Catholics can rest easy knowing that the Church's ordinary and universal magisterium is free from error and that salvation is guaranteed to those who adhere to the Church's traditional doctrines and remain in a state of grace until the moment of their death. As Christ taught in the Gospel of Matthew, "He who hears you hears Me."[42] In saying that, He was instructing the laity to listen to the priests, bishops, and popes of the Catholic Church.

At the same time, God *has* on occasion allowed priests, bishops, and popes who do not always uphold the Church's traditional teachings to reign in His Church. This has occurred throughout history, but also in recent decades. Instead of submitting to the wisdom that our forefathers passed down to us for centuries, many dissident clergy today promote a modernist, liberal ideology that is leading souls astray. This is why Scripture reminds us to "test all things"[43] and to resist those who preach contrary to what Christ taught.[44]

When this happens, it doesn't mean God's promise that the gates of Hell will not prevail against the Church has been broken. He's still in control. And Catholics can still know what it is He wants from them. They simply need to beg Him for clarity. "Ask and it will be given to you, seek and you will find, knock and the door will be opened," Our Lord says in the Gospel of Matthew.[45]

Those words shouldn't be interpreted to mean that we are forbidden from praying to the saints. Indeed, God has always preferred to work through intermediaries (angels, prophets, etc.) when it comes to guiding His flock. He clearly wants us to seek the assistance of those holy men and women that He raised up in Church history. Far from taking away from God's glory, we do Him a great justice when we ask the saints for favors.

41 John 16:13   42 Luke 10:16   43 1 Thessalonians 5:21
44 Galatians 1:8   45 Matthew 7:7

God never leaves us orphaned, even if our clergy sometimes do. Catholics in the 21st century must seek out those religious, both living and dead, like St Alphonsus, who teach the faith in its entirety. May St Alphonsus intercede for us and for God's Church.

ST ALPHONSUS PRAYERS

The following prayers have either been composed by St Alphonsus or by those seeking his assistance. God more readily answers the prayers of holy souls. As a declared saint, Alphonsus reigns in heaven with Him and can intercede for us. Let us beg him to help us with our needs.

For a Greater Love of Jesus and Mary

My glorious and well-beloved patron, St Alphonsus, you have toiled and suffered abundantly to assure men the fruits of the Redemption. Behold the miseries of my poor soul and have pity on me.

By thy powerful intercession with Jesus and Mary, obtain for me true repentance for my sins together with their pardon and remission, a deep hatred of sin, and strength evermore to resist all temptations. Share with me, I pray, at least a spark of that fire of love which your heart always burned. Grant that, following your example, I may make the Will of God the only rule of my life.

Obtain for me also a fervent and lasting love of Jesus, and a tender and childlike devotion to Mary, together with the grace to pray without ceasing and to persevere in the service of God even to the end of my life, that I may finally be united with you in praising God and most holy Mary through all eternity. Amen.

To Unite our Sufferings with Christ

Dear St Alphonsus, friend of the poor, and arthritis sufferer, you are the special patron of all who suffer from arthritis and the pains of many years.

When our joints, hips, arms, legs, and knuckles hurt so much that tears well up in our eyes, help us to recall the tears, the sweat, and the blood that flowed from our crucified Jesus who bore so much suffering out of love for each of us.

St Alphonsus, afflicted with curvature of the spine and nailed to a wheelchair cross in your final years, teach us to unite all our pains with those of Jesus, so our patience and love inspires others to accept the difficulties of their lives.

We ask you to intercede for us so that our pains will be eased but more so that we are enabled to be one with Jesus in his great act of dying and rising. Amen.

Prayer For Healing

Glorious St Alphonsus, loving father of the poor and sick, all your life you devoted yourself with an heroic charity to lightening their spiritual and bodily miseries. Full of confidence in your tender pity for the sick, since you yourself have patiently borne the cross of illness, I come to you for help in my present need (here state your request).

Loving Father of the suffering, St Alphonsus, whom I invoke as the arthritis saint, since you have suffered from this disease in your lifetime, look with compassion upon me in my suffering. Beg God to give me good health. If it is not God's Will to cure me, then give me strength to bear my cross patiently and to offer my sufferings in union with my Crucified Savior and His Mother of Sorrows, for the glory of God and the salvation of souls, in reparation for my sins and those of others, for the needs of this troubled world, and for the souls in purgatory.

Say an *Our Father, Hail Mary,* and *Glory Be.*

St Alphonsus, patron of the sick, pray for me. Amen

Novena to St Alphonsus

Glorious St Alphonsus, Bishop, Confessor, and Doctor of the Church, devoted servant of Our Lord and loving child of Mary, I invoke thee as a saint in heaven. I give myself to thee that thou may always be my father, my protector, and my guide in the way of holiness and salvation.

Aid me in observing the duties of my state of life. Obtain for me great purity of heart and a fervent love of the interior life after thy own example.

Great lover of the Blessed Sacrament and the Passion of Jesus Christ, teach me to love Holy Mass and Holy Communion as the source of all grace and holiness, and to receive this Sacrament as often as I can. Give me a tender devotion to the Passion of my Crucified Redeemer.

Promoter of the truth of Christ in thy preaching and writing, give me a greater knowledge and appreciation of the Divine Truths. Gentle father of the poor and sinners, help me to imitate thy charity toward my fellow men in word and deed. Consoler of the suffering, help me to bear my daily cross patiently in my imitation of thy own patience in thy long illness and to resign myself to the Will of God. Good Shepherd of the flock of Christ, obtain for me the grace of being a true child of Holy Mother Church.

St Alphonsus, I humbly implore thy powerful intercession for obtaining from the Divine Heart of Jesus all the graces necessary for my spiritual and temporal welfare. I recommend to thee in particular this favor (here state your request).

I have great confidence in thy prayers. I earnestly trust that if it is God's Holy Will, my petition will be granted through thy intercession for me at the throne of God.

St Alphonsus, pray for me and for those I love, I beg of thee, by thy love for Jesus and Mary, do not abandon us in our needs. May we experience the peace and joy of thy holy death. Amen.

In thanksgiving to God for the graces bestowed upon St Alphonsus, say the *Our Father, Hail Mary,* and *Glory Be* (three times).

Prayer Before Confession

God of infinite majesty, behold at Thy feet a traitor, who has offended Thee over and over again, but who now humbly seeks forgiveness.

Lord, do not reject me; "A heart contrite and humbled, O God, you will not spurn" (Psalm 51:19). I thank Thee for having waited for me until now and for not letting me die in sin. Since you have waited for me, my God, I hope that by the merits of Jesus Christ you will pardon in this confession all the offenses I have committed against Thee.

I repent and am sorry for them, because by them I have merited hell and lost heaven. But it is not so much on account of hell, but because I have offended Thee, that I am sorry from the bottom of my heart. I love Thee, my Supreme Good, and because I love Thee, I repent of all the insults I have offered Thee. I have turned my back on Thee; I have despised Thy grace and Thy friendship. Lord, I have lost Thee by my own free will.

Forgive me all my sins for the love of Jesus Christ, now that I repent with all my heart. I resolve for the future, by Thy grace, never more willingly to offend Thee. Yes, my God, I would rather die than ever sin again. Amen.

Prayer After Confession

My dear Jesus, how much I owe Thee! By the merits of Thy blood I have this day been pardoned. I thank Thee.

Thou deserve all my love. I will give it all to Thee. I will no longer separate myself from Thee. I have promised You this already; now I repeat my promise of being ready to die rather than offend Thee again.

I promise also to avoid all occasions of sin. My Jesus, Thou knowest my weaknesses; give me grace to be faithful to Thee until death and to have recourse to Thee when I am tempted.

Most holy Mary, help me. You are the Mother of perseverance; I place my hope in thee. Amen.

To Obtain Constancy in Prayer

Eternal Father, for the love of Jesus Christ, let me never fail to recommend myself to Thee whenever I am tempted. I know You always help me when I have recourse to Thee; but my fear is that I may forget to recommend myself to Thee, and my negligence will be the cause of my ruin.

By the merits of Jesus Christ, give me grace to pray to Thee. But grant me such an abundant grace that I may always pray, and pray as I ought!

My Mother Mary, whenever I have had recourse to thee, thou have obtained for me the help which has kept me from failing! Now I come to beg thee to obtain a still greater grace, that of recommending myself always to thy Son and to thee in all my times of need.

My Queen, you obtain all you desire from God by the love you bear for Jesus Christ. Obtain for me now this grace which I beg of thee: to pray always and never to cease praying until I die. Amen.

For the Graces Necessary for Salvation

Eternal Father, Thy Son has promised that Thou will grant us all the graces which we ask for in His name. In the name and merits of Jesus Christ, I ask the following graces for myself and for all mankind.

Please give me a lively faith in all that the Church teaches. Enlighten me that I may know the vanity of the goods of this world and the immensity of the infinite good that Thou art. Make me also see the deformity of the sins I have committed, that I may humble myself and detest them as I should.

Give me a firm confidence of receiving pardon for my sins, holy perseverance, and the glory of heaven, through the merits of Jesus Christ and the intercession of Mary.

Give me a great love for Thee that will detach me from the love of this world and of myself, so that I may love none other but Thee.

I beg of Thee a perfect resignation to Thy Will. I offer myself entirely to Thee, that Thou might do with me and all that belongs to me as Thou pleaseth.

I beg of Thee a great sorrow for my sins.

I ask of Thee to give me the spirit of true humility and meekness, that I may accept with peace and even with joy all the contempt, ingratitude, and ill-treatment I may receive. At the same time, I also ask of Thee to give me perfect charity, which shall make me wish well to those who have done evil to me.

Give me love for the virtue of mortification, by which I may chastise my rebellious senses and oppose my self-love. Give me a great confidence in the Passion of Jesus Christ and in the intercession of Mary Immaculate. Give me a great love for the Blessed Sacrament, and a tender devotion and love to Thy Holy Mother. Give me, above all, holy perseverance and the grace always to pray for it, especially in time of temptation and at the hour of death.

Finally, I recommend to Thee the holy souls of purgatory, my relatives and benefactors, and in a special manner I recommend to Thee all those who hate me or who have in any way offended me; I beg thee to render them good for the evil they have done or may wish to do to me. Grant that, by Thy goodness, I may come one day to sing Thy mercies in Heaven; for my hope is in the merits of Thy blood and in the patronage of Mary. Mary, Mother of God, pray to Jesus for me. Amen.

For Protection from Mary

O Mother of God, Queen of angels and Hope of men, give ear to the one who calls upon thee and has recourse to thy protection.

Behold me this day prostrate at thy feet. I, a miserable slave of hell, devote myself entirely to thee. I desire to be forever thy servant. I offer myself to serve and honor thee to the utmost of my power during the whole of my life. I know that the service of one so vile and miserable can be no honor to thee, since I have so previously offended Jesus, thy Son, and my Redeemer. But if thou wilt accept one so unworthy for thy servant, and by thy intercession change me, and thus make me worthy, this very mercy will give thee that honor which so miserable a wretch as I can never give thee. Receive me, then, and reject me not, O my Mother.

The Eternal Word came down from heaven to earth to seek for lost sheep, and to save them He became thy Son. And when one of them goes to thee to find Jesus, wilt thou despise it? The price of my salvation is already paid; my Savior has already shed His blood, which suffices to save an infinity of worlds. This blood has only to be applied even to such a one as I am.

And that is thy office, O Blessed Virgin; to thee does it belong, as I am told by St Bernard, to dispense the merits of this blood to whom thou pleaseth. To thee does it belong, says St Bonaventure, to save whomsoever thou willest. Help me, my Queen; my Queen, save me. To thee do I this day consecrate my whole soul; do thou save it. Amen.

To Obtain Perseverance Until Death

Eternal Father, I humbly adore and thank Thee for having created me and for having redeemed me. I thank Thee for having made me a Christian by giving me the true faith and for adopting me as Thy child in Baptism.

I thank Thee for having given me time to repent after my many sins, and for having pardoned all my offenses.

I renew my sorrow for them, because I have displeased Thee. I thank Thee also for having preserved me from falling again, as I would have done if Thou had not held me up and saved me. But my enemies do not cease fighting against me, nor will they until I die.

If you do not help me continually, I will lose Thy grace again. I, therefore, pray for perseverance until death.

Thy Son Jesus has promised that Thou will give us whatever we ask for in His name. By the merits of Jesus Christ, I beg Thee, for myself and for all those who are in Thy grace, the grace of never more being separated from Thy love. May we always love thee in this life and in the next. Mary, Mother of God, pray to Jesus for me. Amen.

SELECT BIBLIOGRAPHY

Barrielle, Fr Ludovic-Marie. *Rules for Discerning the Spirits: In the Spiritual Exercises of St Ignatius of Loyola*. Kansas City, MO: Angelus Press, 1995.

Jones, Frederick M. "Alphonsus de Liguori: Select Writings." In *The Classics of Western Spirituality*. Mahwah, NJ: Paulist Press, 1999.

Liguori, Alfonso Maria de'. *Preparation For Death: The Complete Works of St Alphonsus*. Volume I. Edited by Eugene Grimm. New York: Benziger Brothers, 1926.

———. *The Way of Salvation and of Perfection: The Complete Works of St Alphonsus*. Volume II. Edited by Eugene Grimm. New York: Benziger Brothers, 1926.

———. *The Great Means of Salvation and Perfection: The Complete Works of St Alphonsus*. Volume III. Edited by Eugene Grimm. New York: Benziger Brothers, 1927.

———. *The Holy Eucharist: The Complete Works of St Alphonsus*. Volume VI. Edited by Eugene Grimm. New York: Benziger Brothers, 1934.

———. *The True Spouse of Jesus Christ: The Complete Works of St Alphonsus*. Volumes X and XI. Edited by Eugene Grimm. New York: Benziger Brothers, 1926.

———. *Dignity and Duties of the Priest: The Complete Works of St Alphonsus.* Volume XII. Edited by Eugene Grimm, CSSR. New York: Benziger Brothers, 1927.

———. *Preaching: Letter to a Religious. Letter to a Bishop. The Exercises of the Missions. Instructions on the Commandments and the Sacraments: The Complete Works of St Alphonsus Liguori.* Volume XV. Edited by Eugene Grimm, CSSR. New York: Benziger Brothers, 1888.

———. *The 12 Steps to Holiness and Salvation.* Adapted by Cornelius J. Warren, CSSR. Rockford, IL: TAN Books, 1986.

———. *The Glories of Mary.* Revised by Robert A. Coffin. Rockford, IL: TAN Books, 1977.

———. *The Practice of the Love of Jesus Christ.* Translated by Peter Heinegg. Liguori, MO: Liguori Publications, 1997.

———. *Select Writings and Prayers of Saint Alphonsus.* Adopted by John Steingraeber. Liguori, MO: Liguori Publications, 1997.

———. *Sermons of St Alphonsus: For All Sundays of the Year.* Rockford, IL: TAN Books, 1982.

———. *Uniformity with God's Will.* Charlotte, NC: TAN Books, 2012.

———. *Visits to the Blessed Sacrament and the Blessed Virgin Mary.* Charlotte, NC: TAN Books, 2012.

Lodi, Enzo. *Saints of the Roman Calendar.* Translated by Jordan Aumann New York: Alba House, 1992.

Lovasik, Fr Lawrence G. *Saint Alphonsus: The Arthritis Saint.* Tarentum, PA, 2011.

Miller, CSSR, D.F. and L.X. Aubin, CSSR. *Saint Alphonsus Liguori: Doctor of the Church*. Charlotte, NC: TAN Books, 2012.

"St Alphonsus Liguori." Redemptorists International: Scala News. Accessed 12 September 2015. https://www.cssr.news/2015/09/st-alphonsus-liguori/.

About the Author

Stephen Kokx is a journalist for *LifeSiteNews*. A former community college instructor, he has written and spoken extensively about spirituality, Catholic social teaching, and politics. Previously, he worked for the Archdiocese of Chicago. His essays have appeared in a variety of outlets, including *Catholic Family News* and *CatholicVote.org*.